STORES

OF THE YEAR 8

Edited by Martin M. Pegler, SVM

RETAIL REPORTING CORPORATION • NEW YORK

Retail Reporting Corporation
302 Fifth Avenue
New York, NY 10001

Distributors to the trade in Canada
Keng Seng Enterprises, Inc.
4030 rue St. Ambroise, Suite 227
Montreal, Quebec, Canada H4C 2C7

Distributors outside the United States and Canada
Hearst Books International
1350 Avenue of the Americas
New York, NY 10019

Library of Contress Cataloging in Publication Data:
Stores of the Year / 8

Printed and Bound in Hong Kong
ISBN 0-934590-60-5

Designed by Bernard Schleifer

CONTENTS

INTRODUCTION

Store Design, today, is an international expression. Gone are the days when there were cultural or artistic barriers separating one country's retail design concepts from another's. Today we live in a small world — an immediate world — a world without walls, borders or self-serving, jingo-istic attitudes.

It probably began, as most things do, as a simple "borrowing" or an exchange of ideas. European designers of haute couture moved into the U.S. in the 1990s and '80s and introduced us to the store design concepts and store fixturing and furnishing styles that were then favored in the boutiques of Paris, London, Rome and Milan. We liked what we saw and we "adapted" or "adopted" what we liked and added our own "beat" — our own rhythm to satisfy our own retail needs. For years, the European and Asian countries have beckoned to American architects and store designers to come over and design their department stores because for many years the American designers were unequaled in the design, layout and fixturing of mass retail areas. The tri-annual Euroshop, in Dusseldorf, became the place where the Europeans, the Asians and the North, Central and South Americans came together to see — to learn — to understand — and to exchange ideas and materials. Soon that Internationalization was apparent at the NADI shows held in New York and at the WAVM shows on the West Coast. With TV and satellites spinning around us — with images flashing before us within only seconds or two of their happening, the world market narrowed down to the market right outside your store.

In this issue of Stores of the Year, we recognize just how international the Store Design field has become. We present an array of stores and shops located in the U.S., Canada, England, Germany, Austria, The Scandinavian countries, Netherlands, Switzerland, Japan, Brazil, and the Asian countries. The designers and architects whose works are represented in this volume are all part of the Who's Who in Retail Store Design. We are showing stores designed in Europe by American designers as well as European prototypes created by American design firms. One famous Swiss store was designed by an English design firm and fixtured and fitted by a German fixture manufacturer. That is Internationalization!

Shop fittings, modular fixtures and furnishings and concepts that were once considered "European" are now part of our international design language, just as Visual Merchandising and Display techniques advanced by the U.S. designers are now appearing in foreign venues. Lighting and lamps are also international in scope though we still find that how they are used will depend, somewhat, on the customs and shopping traditions of the shoppers in the individual countries.

As in our previous editions, we feature top designer and internationally famous "brand name" boutiques and shops, but we have also included excellent popular priced shops. Some of these are prototypes for chain operations, well established in malls across the country — but putting on a new face. We have lifted special departments or shops out from noted department stores and included them in specific chapters of the book such as the new Casual Women's floor at Bloomingdale's, the Men's Shop at Saks Fifth Ave., and the Home Furnishings area in De Bijenkorf and Harrods. Wherever and whenever possible we have tried to include a facade of the shop and a floor plan or schematic drawing explaining the layout of the fixtures on the floor and the traffic pattern.

This is truly an international tour of retail design and one you don't need a passport to enjoy. You can also leave your camera at home since we are providing some great shots of memorable stores and just enough "guide-talk" to explain it all. Have a fun trip!

MARTIN M. PEGLER

STORES

OF THE YEAR 8

Women's Shops

LANVIN

Rue du Faubourg St. Honore, Paris, France

"Lanvin, the Paris fashion house, established in 1914, wanted a new retail identity that would continue to reflect its heritage but appeal to a younger and more style-conscious customer." The Anglo-French team of Euro RSCG Design Group took a two-pronged approach to solving their client's problem. A concept was developed, based on historical visual elements (originally conceived by the designer of the building, Armand Albert Rateau) which could be applied to furniture, fixtures and fittings in Lanvin's worldwide outlets. A more "architecturally based solution" was taken for the Paris flagship stores which called for a complete internal reorganization.

The women's store, illustrated here, had voids cut through the building to allow for more effective circulation and for greater visual impact both from the street and within the shop. There are two levels which cover 350 sq. meters (about 3,000 sq. ft.) and they were treated by the designers in a "sophisticated and theatrical" manner.

Design: Euro RSCG Design Group, London / Paris
Project Designer: Kenny Holmes / Steve Arnold
Consultant: Terence Conran
Photographer: Jean Philippe Caulliez

A large central space — like an atrium — extends up past the mezzanine level and a smart looking glass and metal bridge spans over the main floor of the space. The area is finished in rich materials and textures but is quite neutral in color. Softly rounded fixtures and fittings contrast with the straight contemporary lines of the wall cabinets and the columns — many of which are either sheathed or outlined with fine woodworking. An Art Deco feeling — truly French in attitude and inspiration — seems to prevail throughout in the styling, the detailing and the furnishing of the space. Note the patterned carpets laid over the white marble floors.

In addition to the many incandescent downlights, the gently vaulted ceilings are illuminated by lights hidden in the coves; some are tinted blue to create a sky-like effect. Both this women's store and the men's store, across the street, were designed and implemented in one year. This meant totally restructuring the buildings internally and externally, plus inventing and designing the new display and presentation systems together with the design of all other items of furnishing and fittings — right down to the ironmongery.

GIANFRANCO FERRE BOUTIQUE

Madison Avenue, New York, NY

Architects: Carruzza, Rancatti & Riva
Ezio Riva, Principal
Stephen Potters, Architects
Stephen Potters, Principal
Tom Clapper, Project Architect
Photographer: Roy Wright Photography, Inc.,
  New York, NY

Adhering to the style of other Ferre shops around the world and on most fashion streets, is this new addition to New York City's Madison Avenue. The store's design is the joint effort of the Italian firm, Carruzza, Rancati & Riva, and the New York firm of Stephen Potters Architects. This store represents the internationally renowned women's wear designer's first venture in New York.

The store contains 3,500 sq. ft. of sales space on the street level and an additional 1,800 sq. ft. for offices, alterations and storage below the street level. The new facade is a recreation of the original building's bronze-work and "it contextually extends to the adjacent Yves St. Laurent showroom."

According to the New York design firm, "The interior is at once sleek, contemporary, luxurious and spacious without disregarding function." The display fixtures and fittings include chrome and steel hanging fixtures for apparel and lacquered columns and showcase walls as well as freestanding chrome and glass cylinders for jewelry and accessories. Surface treatments incorporate gray silver metallic and eggshell wall units which contrast with the pink plastered walls. Polished off-white, lacquered stone is laid on the floor and it is offset with pink, gray and beige carpets.

The rear area of the boutique can be closed off by a lacquered sliding partition to create a private show area with a separate dressing room.

General Contractor: Americon, Inc., New York, NY
Fixtures / Custom Millwork: Siciliano, Arredamenti,
  Bologna
Cabinetwork: Alpine Store Equipment,
  Long Island City, NY

CHRISTIAN LACROIX

Sloane St., London, England

The below street level of the shop is characterized by "the flavor, imagery, classical influences and visual vocabulary of southern France, Provence and Spain."

Design: Caulder Moore Design Consultants, Windsor, Berks, U.K.

The narrow store on Sloane St. is immediately distinguished by the black arabesque framework that fills in and connects the two arched windows at either side of the rectangular entrance. In contrast to the golden interior — the facade is jet black.

The upper level of the narrow shop with the staircase leading to the lower level.

The design firm was appointed to "directly interpret the international Lacroix store image which is characterized by the flavor, imagery, classical influences, and visual vocabulary of southern France, Provence and Spain." The result is an impression of a "sun-drenched, colorful, vibrant intensity within a classical baroque setting."

To achieve the desired effect, the designers worked with the Lacroix "signature colors" — fuchsia, pink, and gold. Throughout the small, two-level shop there is a feeling of opulence and luxury effected by the fuchsia pink fabrics and the gold lavishly applied to fixtures, furniture and interior details. With these colors, Caulder Moore also used light sycamore wood which is kind of "golden" and yellow washed patinate walls: "to highlight the color, seductiveness and details of the merchandise."

To contrast with these brilliant colors black was introduced — especially in an arabesque motif which is reminiscent of a Moorish "exotic mystique" but also providing strength and drama to the interior.

The ground floor and the lower level which are connected by a dramatic stairway outlined in black are only 1000 sq. ft. combined, yet the overall impression is of something larger. The designer's ready-to-wear collection and accessories are displayed in this Sloane St. store — geared towards that special up-scaled, trend-oriented market.

According to the designers, Caulder Moore, "In relief to the prevalence of the cool, lack of passion in many of London's minimalist designer shops — the Lacroix salon is uninhibitedly "maximalist.""

SONIA RYKIEL

Blvd. St. Germain, Left Bank, Paris, France

Design: Euro RSCG Design Agora Sopha, Paris, France
Principal in Charge: Roland de Leu
Project Designers: Steve Arnold & Jeanette Menasce

In the heart of St. Germain des Pres, the mecca of Parisian intellectual life, is Sonia Rykiel's new company headquarters and flagship store. It is located in an 18th century building on the vital corner of Blvd. St. Germain and rue des Saint-Peres.

While respecting the character and architecture of the building, the architects increased the internal space of the building from 1,500 sq. meters (about 13,500 sq. ft.) to 2,000 sq. meters (18,000 sq. ft.) by raising one floor level and creating another intermediary floor. The store itself measures 500 sq. meters (4,500 sq. ft.) and it takes up the ground floor and a wide mezzanine above it. The tall display windows of the shop face out onto the two heavily trafficked streets.

The store is laid out in a succession of different sized spaces around an impressive "conservatory" in what was originally the building's courtyard. The shopper enters through what was once the original, imposing carriage entrance — "reinforcing the feeling of a noble residence."

On the left, a "boutique-type display area displays the whole range of fashion accessories. On the right is a "calmer" and more spacious area for evening wear. The bulk of the Rykiel collection is spread around the "conservatory" and on the wide mezzanine. In the "conservatory — a wide staircase unfurls from the centre of a spectacular 'colorama' of knitwear."

The decoration was designed to be both contemporary and "cozy"; "using a language of shapes, colors and materials from a timeless trend — all in the unmistakable Sonia Rykiel spirit." Natural oak, black carpets and black lacquered steel structures together with refined shapes and a few details which recall the architectural heritage of the building have all made up "an authentic, original concept — strong enough to be applied immediately to all the brand's points of sale."

ST. JOHN BOUTIQUE

Americana Mall, Manhasset, NY

Design: Mathias Thoerner Designs, Munich & New York
Project Architect: Caterina Roiatti
Visual Merchandising: Steve Cheroske
Millwork: Ontario Store Fixtures
Photographer: Andrew Bordwin

The St. John Company of California, working closely with Mathias Thoerner Designs of New York, has developed a store design concept which has been used in the last year in six different stores opened in the U.S. and Europe. "The new St. John system allows the customer an immediate image and product identification — treats each department (reception, sportswear, jewelry, shoes and accessories, evening and lounge) as a complete unit comprising typical configuration, fixtures, finishes and merchandising concept."

For the Manhasset, NY store in the very upscaled Americana Mall, the designers have organized the plan as a sequence of spaces differentiated enough to allow separate department identification and "to keep the customer interested." However, the design is open enough to allow for the shopper to see the focal point of the store — the Oval room for evening wear which is located in the rear of the space.

Limestone and rifted oak with black and chrome accents are used in the store to provide "a very clean and sleek background" for the merchandise. The neutral range of materials was also chosen to maintain a clear image identification for the very large number of furnishing pieces that are part of this new St. John program. In order to get the most out of the merchandise and the setting, the designers selected a combination of high pressure sodium lighting fixtures, low voltage and fluorescent lamps to provide a warm mixture of ambient and accent lighting.

PRINCIPLES

Harlequin Centre, Watford Junction, England

Design: Davies / Baron, London, England

This new prototype store in the Harlequin Centre — located just outside of London — will set the precedent for the gradual change over of the Principle stores throughout the British Isles.

The architects/designers, Davies/Baron, were asked to create a setting for Principle's new signature collection with its emphasis on "simplicity, comfort, purity of design, and uncompromising quality, and to create a simple, open environment that would give the clothes prominence."

The pivotal theme of the store "is the balance set by simple rectangular frames which punctuate and establish equilibrium throughout — from the floor and merchandise bays to the shop front and display cabinets." Natural materials, the attention to details, and the sophisticated, neutral color palette that was affected all provide a perfect background for the merchandise.

Full height glazing on a deep frame and the simple cream marble sign, on the facade, create an immediate sense of openness and accessibility. The displays are unpropped; the merchandise is shown either on dressmaker forms or on bars suspended from the ceiling of the window space. The floors on the interior are finished with dark oak and a sisal matting. On top of these materials are set the white oak display tables which are accented and framed in the dark oak. The garments are shown in simple, flat lay-down arrangements rather than the usual piles of folded garments. The merchandise bays along the walls are also treated simply with "key garments being positioned as 'heroes' to highlight their quality and exclusivity." Black and white fashion photographs by Mikael Jansson are used throughout

the space to "enhance the mood" and show the garments in lifestyle settings.

At the rear of the store is a display area backed up by a grid patterned oak unit and the dressing rooms are located to either side of it. In the center rectangle of the store — on the right — is the large cash/wrap desk which is open and approachable. It has "a domestic (residential) feel" with a large antique display cabinet behind in which accessories can be displayed.

Davis/Baron also designed the graphics package for Principles: "A neutral colored palette and high quality materials, including opulent corded carrier bags, extend the image of the store — customers take an element of Principles home with them."

CARON CHERRY

Bal Harbour Shops, Bal Harbour, FL

Design: Studio Morsa, New York, NY
Antonio Morello / Donato Savoie, Architect
Contractor: RCC Construction
Photographer: Eduard Hueber,
Architectural Photographer

In the very upscaled Bal Harbour — in the truly upscaled Bal Harour Shops is this new 1,000 sq. ft. shop, Caron Cherry, a women's clothing store specializing in refined contemporary clothing. The merchandise is an interesting collection of name brand and designer fashions.

According to the design firm, "the small store is constructed of simple, ordinary materials — exquisitely finished." Contrasting with the soft fabrics and the innovative designs are materials like sandblasted steel burnished with graphite, polished concrete and hammered metal alloys. Because the merchandise is not only seasonable but changeable in product lines, the store had to be easy to change about and rearrange. At one time there may be many shoes on display while at other times there is a profusion of little black dresses. To accommodate this, all but the long steel and glass display rack and the dressing rooms are movable and can be rearranged to highlight specific products. The groups of square steel tables can be moved and reassembled also.

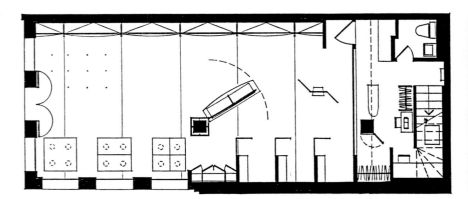

The clothing and accessories can be displayed on a series of steel rods that are fitted into a grid of recessed floor plugs. Elements can be added to or removed from the wall display and the patterned glass wall obscures without hiding the dressing rooms and office/alteration area in the rear.

The lighting is all reflected light which is flattering to both the merchandise and the affluent customers.

LIZ CLAIBORNE

Somerset Collection, Troy, MI

Design: HTI / Space Design International, New York, NY

This new 8,400 sq. ft. shop in the Somerset Collection in Troy, MI was designed to showcase the Liz Claiborne collection in a space as "comfortable and contemporary" as the clothing being shown. The space supports the whole range of the Liz Claiborne line: career wear, casual wear, dresses, suits, shoes, hosiery, hats, accessories, jewelry, and fragrances. According to the designers, "by presenting coordinated outfits in a series of well merchandised displays, the retail environment shows the clothing to its best advantage and encourages shoppers to make multiple purchases."

HTI/SDI created a space with partial walls which both segment the merchandise and yet also allow the retailer to expand or contract the various collections with each new season. As a backdrop for the merchandise, the designers used light woods with a color palette mainly cream and ivory. Natural light oak was used for the flooring and the custom designed fixtures. The feature walls are covered with either a special sponge paint treatment, natural oak with brushed stainless steel reveals or silk tussah fabric.

The Liz Claiborne signature colors that also appear on the packaging and graphics are used in the store's design: bright yellow aniline dyed wood cover the columns that flank the entrance, red columns and seating inside along with the bright blue mirror enframements.

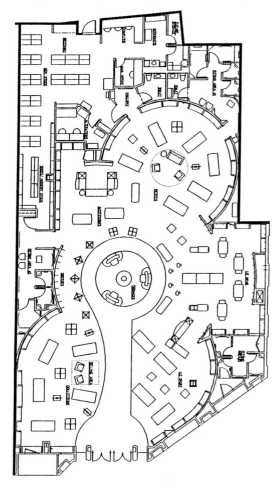

The open plan of the shop offers unobstructed views "enabling the customers to see the full range of merchandise on display." Focal walls are dramatically lit and well displayed with coordinated outfits. The curved shape of the display walls is repeated in the ceiling and on the floor — "giving definition to the various departments and providing a sense of intimacy." Honed stone floor patterns mark the aisles and the furniture, fixtures and area rugs are used to break up the sales floor and create a relaxed, residential feeling that encourages browsing.

This new prototype design will be implemented in future Liz Claiborne shops.

CASUAL CORNER

Hickory Point Mall, Decatur, IL

Design: Jon Greenberg Associates, Southfield, MI

Casual Corner stores appear in hundreds of malls across the U.S. and this new store in Decatur, MI is a departure for the popular priced chain. According to the design firm, the design inspiration for this store came from the spacial relationships as expounded and demonstrated in the work of Frank Lloyd Wright. Materials were chosen in the Wright tradition — from nature: from the limestone used on the storefront, the entrance and to ornament the cash wrap desk to the warm woods used throughout the space on walls and floors. A terrazzo floor proves most serviceable at the entrance and carpets are used in the main merchandise area.

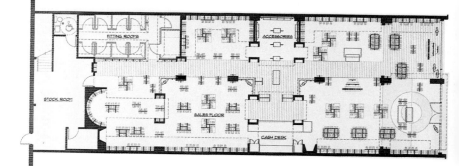

The customers enter through a low entry. Next to the entry is a colonnade that runs the length of the store creating displays along the columns that form the corridor. Some columns are equipped with stubbed face-outs to showcase a garment while other columns support modular display units to showcase the merchandise. Throughout the store alternating intimate the open spaces divide the store.

In the front of the store JGA took different approaches to walls, furniture and fixtures. Slot-wall carries out the line of the window mullions — spaced in the same dimensions as the store front. Then, turning the corner — wing walls create alcoves or display rooms "each with its own mood." The simple and straightforward fixtures are champagne-colored nickel-aluminum finished to match the slot-wall. Among the custom fixtures are two stepped racks with six fixed vertical posts to showcase several turnouts simultaneously; a coordinate fixture of wood and metal; and a table of wood, metal, and glass.

The accessories area is a blend of wood with champagne colored slot walls. It is set under low ceilings and adjacent to the colonnade which makes it a cross axis for the store. At the center of the store, L-shaped partitions — patterned after the glass in the storefront — echo the entrance design on the interior.

The ceiling appears to float overhead and the track lighting is hidden from view. Throughout the lighting is HID white sun for "better merchandise contrast and color."

BLOOMINGDALES

2nd Floor, Lexington Ave., New York, NY

Design: Walker Group / CNI, New York, NY

Bloomingdales called upon Walker Group/CNI to clearly define and refine the circulation on the second floor of its flagship store on Lexington Ave. in New York City. While consolidating merchandise from other floors, Bloomingdales also wanted "a unique and cohesive look" for this, their Moderate Sportswear floor.

The architectural/design firm's solution included flexible environments for the vendor shops on this floor. This allows the store's management to add, subtract, or even combine spaces when necessary while at the same time "maintaining a unified architectural element throughout the floor." The all-important circulation on this floor is driven by the strong curved aisle plan which is distinguished by different flooring materials. "It continuously moves the customers around the floor in a clear, easy-to-understand manner."

Light, natural colors and materials were used to create the effect of a "beach house" — a kind of casual but elegant atmosphere. Interestingly, environmentally sound, non-endangered products were utilized.

Walker Group/CNI featured original architectural elements and details of this handsome Art Deco building to enhance the newly conceived retail environment. Windows to the outside were uncovered and "a banner of clerestory windows were created to give additional light — an open feeling and also unify the entire floor."

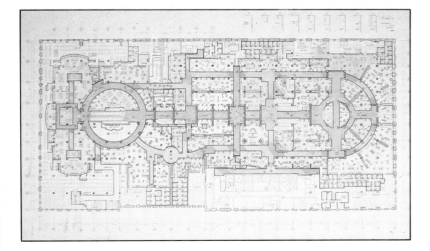

GRAND-JURY

Wildwood Manor, Bethesda, MD

Design: The Office of Alexia N.C. Levite, Washington, DC

The challenge to the design firm was to convert the long narrow space of 1,700 sq. ft. with a later added-on additional 700 sq. ft. into a "gallery-like craft-art and women's clothing store." The store had to have a flexible display system that would accommodate not only clothing and accessories but artwork as well. Additionally, the space would have to provide "a comfortable shopping experience for both women and men."

In order to draw the customers through the space, an eye-catching focal display presentation was designed to dominate the rear end wall. In addition, a cove-lit, tent shaped ceiling helps to draw one's attention down the length of the store to the rear. By balancing the artwork which is located in continuous niches along one side wall with the clothes and jewelry displays along the opposite wall, the trip through the store is made interesting — and different. In order to maintain flexibility, the niches were designed using the same display system as in other areas of the store. These niches were designed to hold artwork, clothing, or accessories — as needed. Not only do the niches provide framed display areas, but when the store was expanded they were removed to allow access into the new additional space.

Throughout the neutral space the designer used lacquer on poplar wood, drywall construction, plastic laminates, carpet and mirror. All the millwork was custom designed and the design firm also created the display table and jewelry cases used in the expansion area.

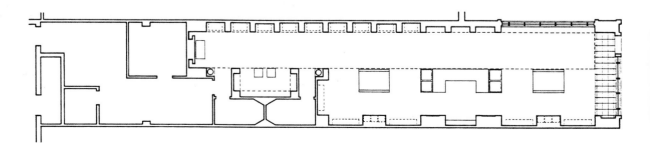

VIVA VIDA BOUTIQUE

Morumbi S/C, Sao Paulo, Brazil

Design: A+E Arquitetura
Photographer: Nelson Khon

The left hand wall (right). Just in front of the entrance one can see the backs of the TV monitors and the sweeping curve of stainless steel that supports the shoulder-out hung garments.

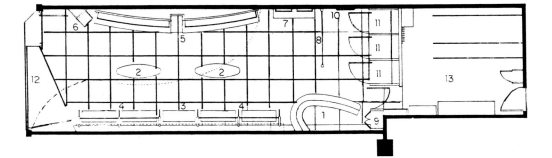

In keeping with the new imaging of the company through its showroom as shown on the previous pages — here we present one of the four stores recently completed that introduce that new look where the public meets the garments.

In the Morumbi S/C — "the clear shades and the curves of the forms bring the idea of femininity and the sophistication of their clothes" into the interior of the shop.

The space is narrow and long and thus afforded the designers the opportunity to cut off an area for stock in the very far end of the space (#13). Typical of mall presentations, Viva Vida does have a large area, up front, behind the tall glass window for the display of featured garments. The soft curves that added so much to the look of the showroom are echoed here in the sweep of the curved hanging fixtures along the left wall (#5) and in the elongated oval display tables on the floor that follow the line of the space and also move the shopper gently towards the rear of the store. The horse shoe shaped cash/wrap desk (#1) is located at the end of the shop near the three, amply proportioned dressing rooms which are next to the entrance into the stockroom. A large frosted glass screen (#8) serves as a demarcation between the selling floor and the try-on area beyond.

Along the right hand wall of the store is a modular fixture concept that combines shelves with face-out hanging. The elliptical shape of the glass-topped tables (#2) is repeated on the fins that support the shelves and hang rods against the off-white walls. Besides some black accents, the other "color" in this no-color set-up is the brushed stainless steel curved wall (#5) — which also recalls the arced stainless panels that camouflaged the columns in the Viva Vida showroom.

Focusable spots with warm incandescent lamps light up the interior along with the recessed, hidden fluorescents that illuminate the side perimeter walls and the merchandise. Up front — and seen from the mall is a wall of stacked TV monitors that play the fashion tapes and promotional materials previewed by the buyers in the showroom.

A view from the entrance (above). TV monitors play fashion shows and promotional tapes up front and elongated oval shapes appear on the free standing tables and as the dividers and hang-rod supporters on the wall on the right.

A close-up on the wall merchandising module. The fins support the shelves or hang rods. The long oval, glass-topped tables carry a display of fashion accessories below and the top shelf is used to show merchandise and coordinate outfits.

CHARMANTE

Montreal, Quebec, Canada

Design: Gervais Harding, Montreal, Quebec
Photographer: Yves Lefebvre, Montreal, Quebec

The target market for this chain of stores located in Montreal and Quebec City is "the fashionable working woman." This particular store is located in a large regional mall and though the store has a 25 ft. linear frontage in the "fashion alley" of the mall, the store is 100 ft. deep. Part of the design firm's problem was to eradicate the "bowling alley" curse of the plan and still design a store that would be "easily identifiable and very inviting." It was important that the store front have a high impact effect and by raising the mall's bulkhead structure, they were able to achieve a dramatic 13 ft. high facade.

In order to avoid the "bowling alley" configuration, the store plan was devised so that the back of the store seems "to veer off around the corner." Several commodious changing rooms are banked at an odd angle to one back corner and another smaller cluster is located just into the store opposite the cash/wrap which is set at an acute angle. "This visually creates distinct areas and ambiences within the boutique — offering ideal opportunities to departmentalize merchandise, create displays and promote collections."

Polished marble floors extend in a long, soft curve from the entrance to the cash/wrap counter. This form is repeated along the ceiling and focuses attention directly into the store." Neutral, sophisticated materials were used to give the "feeling of warmth and to enhance the various selections of clothing." Custom paint finishes were used to create a strong visual statement on the ceiling and in the changing rooms.

By introducing decorative features such as built-in furniture, custom tables, sign panels and an illuminated, curved wood paneled backwall — "a very special environment was created." The built-in units, floor racks and the cash/wrap counter are a harmonious blend of custom mill work and metal work. Brass "tears" were welded onto the twisted gun metal decorative ceiling panels and the showcase legs.

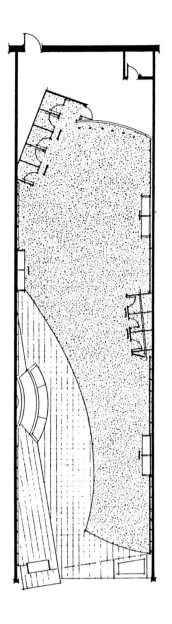

COLETTE / IRO

Les Galeries de la Capitale, Quebec City, Quebec, Canada

Design: Gervais Harding, Montreal
Design Principal: Steve Sutton
Interior Designer: Frank De Niro
Technician: James Lee
Lighting Consultant: Larry Noreyko

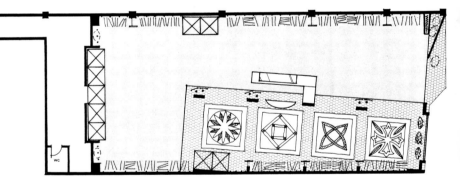

According to the designers of this upscaled women's fashion boutique of 3,000 sq. ft., it is actually a store within a store. The "IRO" part of the store is defined by its cross vaulted ceiling, stone floor with 9'x9' mosaic tile insets, and cable light fixtures. It has a much more intimate ambience than the clean, open look of "COLETTE" — up front.

The facade is a combination of "two distinct store images" even though the shopper must go through the Colette part to get to the Iro shop. Even though the store was designed to have a definite feeling of two separate boutiques, it still functions as a single store. There is a central cash island nestled between a row of pseudo stone clad columns that separate Colette from Iro.

Hammered and honed sandstone is used as the cladding for the facade and also on the interior columns. The stone is also the principal floor finish for the Iro boutique. In addition there are four different mosaic patterns centered under the ceiling vaults and aged and textured paint finishes are used to imitate the weathered painted stone facades of antique European buildings. These finishes are used to accent the vaulted ceiling and the walls around the changing rooms and the display areas. Gervais and Harding has also designed and specified hand-worked, wrought iron details and high quality millwork to harmoniously create the desired ambience for the store.

This prototype design has proven to be an immediate success in the selected market and another store — following the same design program — is already in the works.

MONDAINE

Promenade de L'Outaouasis, Outaouasis, Quebec, Canada

Design: Optima Design, Montreal, Quebec
Contractor: Prisma Construction, Montreal, Quebec
Photographer: Andre Doyon

Mondaine is a rapidly expanding chain of women's specialty stores in Quebec and this store, designed by Optima Design of Montreal, is a prototype for future roll outs. The main mandate from the client was to create a setting that would act as an impressive background for the merchandise without overwhelming it. In order to still add a degree of excitement to the overall design, the store designers played with the non-merchandising areas like the cash/wrap counter and its back unit, the dressing rooms, the ceiling and store front.

In order to eliminate large stretches of wall merchandising, Optima introduced details such as cash counter and structural dressing rooms — creating 12 to 14 foot wall sections in which merchandise color stories can be facilitated. The back end of the store is used as the focal point of the total design and "it visually foreshortens the actual length of the store, thereby attracting people to circulate in the back area." This was accomplished by adding "organic" columns, curved maple wood walls and dropped ceiling details. To stay within the budget restraints, the designers incorporated "large volume" trim with inexpensive "Steptoe & Wife" metal ornament applique details — which also tend to unite the overall shop design.

To contrast with the cold metals, a warm palette of orange and yellow was used to affect "a contemporary environment reflecting the merchandise and the target market."

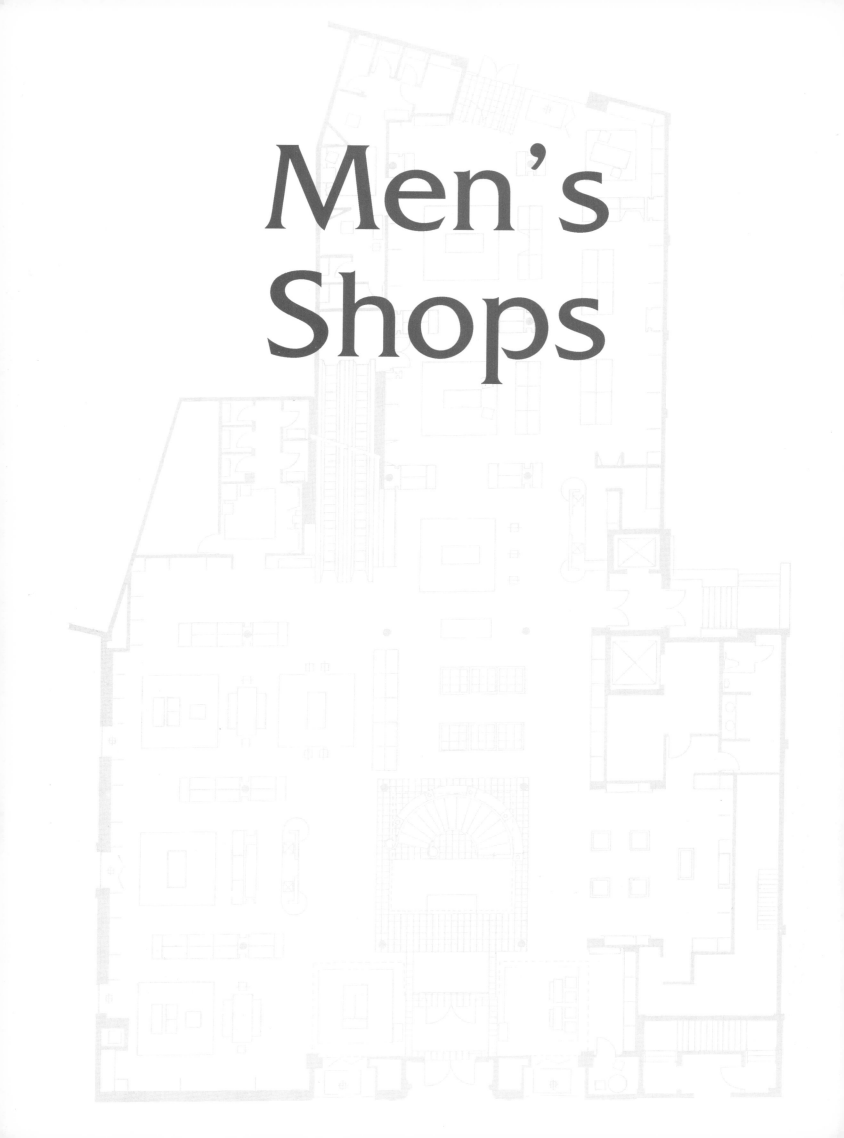

Men's Shops

SAKS FIFTH AVE.

Men's Floor, Fifth Ave., New York, NY

According to the designers, Fitzpatrick Design Group, the brief that was handed to them by Saks Fifth Ave. was quite simple — "create a plan that's easy to shop and merchandise and a design that is updated traditional — and warm."

As is usual for this design firm, "first, as always, we created the form then fit the function." They opened up the windows that look out onto Fifth Ave. and Rockefeller Plaza and thus created the focal "Oval Room" with all its formality. This area anchors the plan and the organization of the merchandising: American clothing to the left — European clothing to the right, and all the Designer Shops in the center. Also, according to the plan and the aisle design, exposure with most shops is guaranteed and most are only 25' deep. The entire floor is extremely well lit and service oriented. There are large fitting rooms strategically placed and well appointed. The high ceilings of this floor recall the graciousness of old time specialty stores.

For design inspiration, Fitzpatrick Design Group just looked out of the newly "opened" windows. The entire floor and "the envelop of design" was inspired partially by the adjacent Art Deco Radio City Music Hall and Rockefeller Plaza, but even more so by Jacques Ruhlmann, the great French traditionalist of "art decorative." From the Normandie — viewed from another window — they drew inspiration for the Fifth Ave. Club — "an elegant reminder of quality and craftsmanship seldom witnessed in decades."

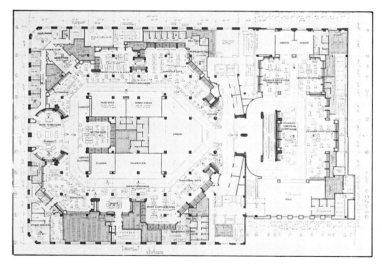

Design: Fitzpatrick Design Group, New York, NY

The pencil striped graining of the Quartered Saelli — the "common denominator" wood in the design — runs horizontally and vertically through the space and adds emphasis to the round columns with white fluted capitals. The travertine marble aisles are bordered by cut and loop pile neutral colored carpets. "The period metal is stainless steel with wood bases and trim."

"This men's floor is special in character — and quite SAKS."

ALFRED DUNHILL OF LONDON

Geneva, Switzerland

Design: Rosenblum / Harb Architects, New York, NY
Principal in charge: Elliot Rosenblum
Project Architect: Marcie Weisberg
Photographer: Robert Miller

Alfred Dunhill has a long and respected history — 100 years to be exact — as a tobacconist and purveyor of men's fashions and fashion accessories. This not un-likely combination of product lines has appeared to-gether across the U.S. and in fashionable European cities. Though tradition and heritage are mainstays of the Dunhill image, Rosenblum/Harb Architects were commissioned to create an "up-dated" look for the Dunhill retail stores. The first of the new design ap-peared in Seattle and this one, in Geneva, is the first European exposure of the new look.

The architect/designers were called upon "to create a setting that would evoke the luxury and sophistication of an urban gentleman's private quarters." They de-signed this store of about 1500 sq. ft. as a modern interpretation of European Art Deco with elegantly panelled walls made of high gloss cherry wood accented and outlined with brushed nickel trim. From outside the store the shopper sees the softly rounded ends of the wood sheathed and glass topped display cases and the wood outlined recessed wall cabinets. Overstuffed leather couches of a rich cognac color complement the wood and the beige carpeting which is bordered with a Greek key design executed in black and terra cotta. The art deco curves that distinguish the wooden cases on the floor is echoed by the circular shape of the cigar room. The individual dressing rooms are located next to this area.

"Custom fixtures in a variety of exotic woods rein-force the atmosphere of a private collection of furnish-ings accrued over the years." Art deco style murals and artwork decorate some of the warm white walls.

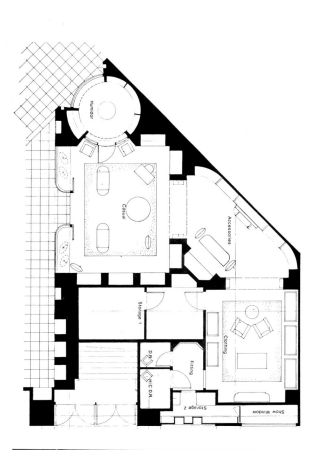

BRUNO MINELLI

Eldorado S/C, Sao Paulo, Brazil

Design: A+E Arquitetura
Photographer: Nelson Khon

The store front facing the main
traffic aisle in the Eldorado S/C.

This Bruno Minelli men's boutique is located in the up-scaled Eldorado S/C and it is one of the five shops A+E has designed for this company. The exterior of the shop is almost entirely glass with only the wide double doorway and over doorway panel accented in black. From the marbled floor of the mall aisle, the shopper can see the entire selling space; the floor laid in a diagonal checker board of natural finished woods — sweeping areas of gray marble patterned with black diamonds — walls that are curved and arced — and a curved shape cut out of the dropped ceiling which is accented with cool fluorescents hidden in the cove and in the soffit.

The challenge was to create "a work of identification of a masculine image — perfectly acknowledged and still in keeping with the merchandise" which happens to be well tailored, sophisticated sports clothes. The store is distinguished by the striking difference of the flooring materials and the textures and materials used on the walls as well as the "designed" and patterned ceiling treatment.

Black dolomite panels create a series of framed merchandise bays where jackets and slacks are hung, shoulder out, and illuminated by the cool lamps hidden beneath the soffit. The upper shelves are saved for displays. The same black finish is used on the multi-tiered tables that are islands of merchandise presentation out in the center of the floor. Shirts, ties and other accessories are neatly folded and presented on these tables.

The dramatic, cove-lit, oval cut-out in the ceiling is repeated on the floor with the oval shaped gray marble design on the wood parquet floor. All around focusable lamps, set in the dropped ceiling, are used to highlight the wall hung merchandise, the displays and the garments laid out on the black and stainless steel tables. The service counter is also finished in the same dark wood and it is set against a frosted glass wall with a recessed curve while the fascia above is curved forward into the selling space. Long shelves, on the right, carry folded garments while the standing mirror, left, separates the selling area from the dressing rooms located on the other side of the large square glass resting on the black oval base.

The store as seen from the entrance. A giant oval design is "cut-out" of the dropped ceiling and the oval shape is repeated in a marble "area rug" on the wood floor. Note the detail of the "cut-out" ceiling.

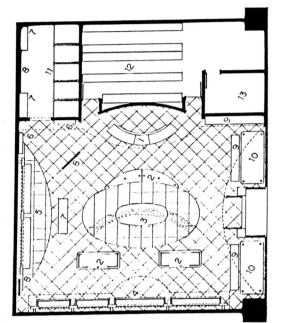

A view to the left of the shop where the jackets are lined up, shoulder out, in the bays created by the black dolomite framework.

The right hand side of the shop with the curved cash/wrap counter set beneath the sweeping curved soffit and the frosted glass wall behind the counter.

A pair of elongated oval glass topped tables (right) with shelves beneath are set out on the black marble trimmed gray oval "rug." Note the detailing of the cut-out ceiling oval.

REALTA

Chicago, IL

Design: Richar Interiors, Chicago, IL
Photographer: Wayne Cable, Cable Studios

The owners of this ultra upscaled men's shop, Glenn Ventura and Mel Camm, somehow hoped to find a designer who would instill the 2,400 sq. ft. store with a warm, romantic ambience. In selecting Richar of Richar Interiors they not only got "romance" but a warm, inviting and truly unique shop with a strong residential feeling.

According to the designer, "We wanted Realta to be much warmer and more inviting than the average retail space so we chose elements that are more typical of residential design than commercial." To contrast with the contemporary styling of the clothing, the designer found his inspiration in the Gothic style and in the Middle Ages and a stained glass palette of royal blue, garnet, ocher gold, and copper. The unique chandeliers that hang down throughout the space have amber glass sides which create a warm, fire-light glow wherever the light touches a surface. Even the heavy floral tapestry fabric used to upholster some of the furniture suggests the romantic, swash-buckling era.

The walls are hand painted and glazed to suggest an antique European heritage and the custom made area rug, used in the main clothing room, looks like a marble mosaic floor in a castle. Faux finishes were cleverly integrated into the space to enhance the desired look — to unify the elements — and also help keep within the budget. The "limestone" table that stands atop the "mosaic" rug is just one good example. Also in this area is the stunning ceiling painted by Roland Montijo and Robert Frank that also suggests the painted wooden ceilings in Spain at the time of El Cid. Across the windows are blue velour drapes pulled back and held with frise fabric tie-backs.

Realta offers more than top designer clothes in an exciting, palatial setting. It offers unique services which include picking up and delivering out-of-town shoppers at the airport, croissants and coffee, light snacks and even a place to shower and change into the just altered clothes before a night out on the town. This is really service!

ARMSTRONG & JONES

Munich, Germany

Design: Mathias Thoerner Designs, Munich &
*   New York, NY*
Project Designer: Rainer Hoffman
Project Architect: Henning Meyer
Contractor: Fraemke & Sons
Photographer: Antje Anders

Located in the main shopping area of Munich, in a 1910 building, is this two story Jones & Armstrong store. The designer, Mathias Thoerner of Munich and New York has created in the 2,800 sq. ft. space, "A classically minimal interior with an eye towards younger customers." However, the combination of elegant simplicity and contemporary sleekness is proving to be appealing to people of all ages.

The exceptional feature of the store is the cross-over bridge between the men's and women's sections which is accentuated by a light grained oak "pier." "Under teal blue portals, it works with the coved ceiling above to intensify the feeling of floating between two disproportionately elevated spaces." Narrow open railings connect the structure to five limestone steps.

Custom cabinets, furniture detailing, decorative moldings and oak planked floors mix with the black steel and maple panel system, and the stainless steel hang bars "offering a vibrant clarity." The merchandise is made more accessible in conventional display units or spread out on tables. A unique, double faced structure offers seating on one side and has shelving arranged on the other side.

To ensure a faithful rendition of color in this men's area, the designers specified high pressure sodium and low voltage halogen lamps. It is a "blend of warm reddish and cooler tones" that present the merchandise to its best advantage.

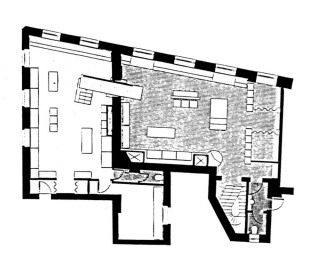

CUZZENS

The Forum Shops, Las Vegas, NV

Design: Brand + Allen Inc., Houston, TX
Design Team: John Allen / Howard Hill
Photography: Jud Haggard

The entrance into Cuzzens and
a view of the first area of the
store where sportswear is
shown. One can see the ornate
fountain and the semi-covered
arcade around the fountain.

Cuzzens is an upscale, Italian Men's clothing store for the contemporary life-style and it makes its first appearance in Nevada in the Forum Shops.

The curved windows on either side of the double doored entrance sort of sweep the shopper into the store. The first impression is of a formal residence in old Rome or Pompeii before the lava spread. The first area of the store which is divided into three parts looks like a large open entry porch including columns, an open roof treatment with clay shingles and a large and impressive fountain in the center — like in an open atrium.

The store is a handsome blend of woods and marbles — of charcoal gray carpeting, white lacquered columns with modified Tuscan caps and accent areas of Pompeiian red — or faded terra cotta.

Various shades of wood are used on the floor tables and fixtures and the Empire style wall cabinets that are topped with semi-circular or triangular pediments of stark white encased and framed in wood. The materials and colors get darker as one progresses through the three distinct areas of the store.

Sportswear is presented up front in the "entry" area where the materials are the lightest. The cashier's desk serves as a break between the second and third areas of the store and each area is further separated by a marble patterned band on the floor and an arcade of columns. The second area is a little more formal than the first and here one can see more formal sportswear and furnishings. The final area is the most "interior" of all and here suits and shoes are displayed. The dressing rooms are also back here. The shoe shop is way off in the rear with an entrance to the shoe storage area. Behind and out of sight is the fully equipped tailor shop.

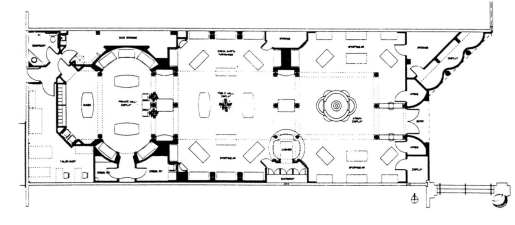

A view from the cash desk (on the left) into the men's suit area and the shoe department in the very rear of the store. Milk glass bowl, pendant fixtures hang down throughout this space to add a warm ambient light while recessed spots provide the balance of the illumination.

Standing at the cash desk and looking across the second area to the shirts and ties displayed on the walls. Notice the inset marble pattern that is used between the space and to accentuate the dividing colonnades.

HACKETT

Sloane St., London, England

Design: Caulder Moore Design Consultants, Windsor, Berks, U.K.

In conjunction with English Heritage, the facade was renovated and the display presentations are simple and "no nonsense."

Located off Sloane Square, on Sloane St. — but at the far end of the street, is another Caulder Moore project which is completely different in concept and look as one can get from the Lacroix salon up nearer to Brompton Rd. This 6000 sq. ft. space is on three levels and the designers have attempted to imbue the space with the image of an exclusive men's club — just right for the exclusive men's outfitters.

The original facade of the building has been essentially maintained and "restored" to a look befitting the shop, the building, and the merchandise. To accomplish this the designers worked closely with "English Heritage" — a landmark commission.

The designers also reclaimed and enhanced the existing mahogany floors, the plaster columns and the ceiling details. The two selling floors (the street level and one flight up) combined have a sales space of about 4300 sq. ft. and they are joined by a sweeping staircase of Portland stone with cast iron balustrades which reflect the overall style of the selling space.

That "style" is rich, masculine and traditional, with finely polished hardwood fixtures and fittings. The dark woods and the subdued lights along with the classic, clean lines of today's retailing create the image desired by Hackett for this, the flagship store. Here is brought together all the individual product areas in one location. In addition to the retail space and a specialist service area, there is a tailor shop and a barber shop.

In summing up what they hoped to accomplish, Caulder Moore tried to create a functional and efficient masculine setting somewhat influenced by the Edwardian style found in banking halls and public lobbies which would appeal to men "not influenced by fashion" — and covering a broad age range in the upper market sector.

According to James Pow, Managing Director of Hackett, this location was selected because, "It has a very interesting customer profile which is in part due to existing retail outlets, quality hotel trade and also the strong residential aspect of this part of Chelsea. Hackett will certainly be setting standards in menswear."

Connecting the two selling floors is a dramatic stairway made of Portland stone with a cast iron balustrade that reflects the overall Hackett "style".

Views of the ground floor level which combines the existing mahogany floors with flagstoned areas. The fixtures, fittings, and furniture are finely finished hardwoods and the lighting is soft and subdued. The overall feeling is of elegance and an Edwardian men's club.

BRITCHES GREAT OUTDOORS

Westfarms Mall, West Hartford, CT

Design: Bergmeyer Associates, Inc., Boston, MA
V.P. Partner in Charge / Planner: Joseph P. Nevin Jr.
Designer: Joseph P. Nevin, Jr. / Doug Coots
Consultant: Richard Altuna, Los Angeles, CA
Retailers Design Team: Philip J. Iosca, President
John Clark, Exec. V.P.
Gene Kellway, Dir. Store
Plan. & Construction
Photographer: Chun Y. Lai, New York, NY

Inspired by the great out-of-doors — and the store's name, the designers of this project, Bergmeyer Associates of Boston, combined elements found in a park service ranger's headquarters with an interior reminiscent of an old New England boat house. The store is targeted mostly at collegiate men and women who will find here seasonal as well as year-round outdoors and athletic fashions.

Working with the design consultant, Richard Altuna of Los Angeles, Bergmeyer developed an interior environment that separates the space into four areas; Outdoorsy, The Rugby Room, The Great Room (for dressier wear) and The Alley (for the basic products). In addition to the outdoors theme, the new prototype design evolved from the segmented design of the client's first store in Georgetown. "A conglomeration of add-on buildings, split levels, and changes in materials and finishes, the store lent itself well to establishing desig-

nated areas for product grouping." In this Westfarms prototype the designers improved upon that concept by coordinating the distribution of natural materials, wood and stone and soffited wall openings with modeled plaster intentionally creating individual merchandising areas. Ceiling timbers and pitched planks, which suggest a boat's keel, add to the New England boat house atmosphere as does the actual rowing shell suspended from the ceiling in The Great Room.

Flexible, customized fixtures were designed "that maintain a signature quality" for the store. A merchandise bay system which incorporates fold down shelves and hang rods along with the large, free standing tables together with other fixtures on the floor meet the merchandising objectives of the client. "Unique to this merchandise system was its minimum spacial requirement and ability to accommodate various shelving configuration for effective product display."

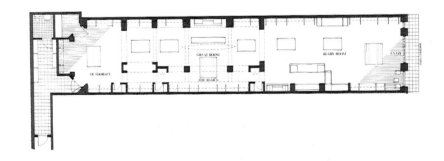

BUTCH GALLERY

Knokke, Belgium

Design: Umdasch Shop-Concepts, Neidenstein
Marc Boname, Belgian Marketing and Planning Bureau

This totally new store of 450 sq. meters (approx. 4750 sq. ft.) on two stories was designed by the Umdasch Shop-Concept Group. It is located in a fine shopping district of the city and caters to upscaled citizens as well as tourists to Knokke. Though Butch Gallery is also a women's wear shop, we are concentrating on the men's area in the store.

The shopper enters into a two story high "atrium" with a handsome creamy stone floor warmed up with richly colored Oriental-type rugs. Directly in front is an imposing stairway constructed and finished with a honey toned, natural wood which leads the shopper up to the mezzanine where the menswear is housed. Squat, square columns sheathed in the warm light wood support the second level and then seem to continue up to the ceiling. A magnificent, ornate chande-lier hangs down over the central space of the shop contrasting with the sharp, clean lines of the store's architecture and fittings. Simple, black iron railings span between the columns on the second level.

The designers used several of the Umdasch fitting and fixturing systems to furnish the mezzanine space. The black metal wall strips hold shelves, hangrods and other accessory units designed to go with the system. The shelves are wood and match the wood mosaic floor and the wooden columns that surround the space. Angled shelves — like magazine racks — are used on the top to show off shirts and ties. The floor fixtures are compatible in design and are constructed of wood trimmed with black metal. The merchandise that is presented on the wall units is beautifully illuminated with MR16s set into swivel bases in the ceiling.

MARK SHALE

Country Club Plaza, Kansas City, MO

Design: Charles Sparks + Company, Westchester, IL
Principal in Charge: Charles Sparks
Project Manager: Don Stone
Project Team: Jim Hanson / Michael Sparks / Michael
  Fleetwood / Rachel Scheu
V.M. for Mark Shale: Jill Kurth
Photographer: James Norris, Chicago, IL

Scott Baskin, the president of Mark Shale stores said, "We are looking for a fresh approach — something that would become the next generation of Mark Shale stores." To create that new look for this chain of stores which offers classic, sophisticated and stylish career and casual merchandise targeted at men and women who view themselves as career professionals, the company selected Charles Sparks + Company to blend modernism with tradition to affect the new store prototype.

The design firm took advantage of the "eclectic, Spanish style architecture and the traditional character of the Country Club Plaza. The opportunities for blending the old and the new were intriguing." However, the challenge was to convert this three level, free standing 56,000 sq. ft. former department store into a multi-tenant use building with Mark Shale occupying a portion of the main and upper levels for selling. A part of the lower level space was reserved for stock, offices and receiving. The company now occupies almost 30,000 sq. ft. of the total space.

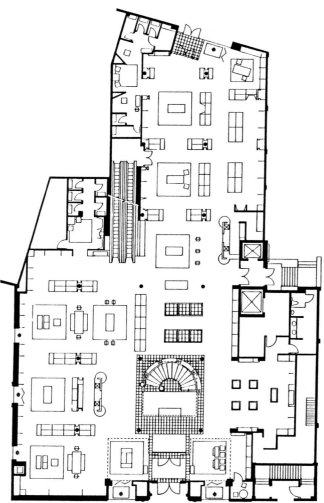

The overall store design inspiration was derived from the "simplicity and functionality found in the works of the early modernists such as Van Der Rohe, Le Corbusier, and Frank Lloyd Wright. The feeling we tried to create was one of sensuous, functional modernism distilling the luxurious simplicity of the '20s and '30s into the '90s." They also had to create a sense of timelessness and permanence while offering total mobility and versatility to all the components in the design including the fixturing. The loose fixture design of the space is able "to communicate a sense of importance and permanence" while allowing for the frequent changes necessitated by the fluctuations in merchandise capacity.

The main organizing principle of the "free plan" was a series of elements which could be rearranged; a series of interlocking rooms arranged loosely in a grid through which there are "avenues," "side streets" and "cul de sacs." The ceiling architecture and lighting plan over-

lay a uniform pattern on the ever-changing fixture plan allowing for lighting virtually any fixture configuration. The fixtures and mill work were simple, planar, rectilinear and panelized with carefully proportioned reveals and void of ornament.

On the mail level where the Men's clothing is located, figured, quarter sliced, anigre veneers were sequence matched to affect the image of high quality executive case goods. Otherwise the interior is monochromatic and consistently planar. Bold patterned rugs act as centerpieces to the room-like spaces set between high "wardrobe" fixtures. The walls that are not covered with the golden wood tones are painted a pale vanilla color. Also incorporated into the texture of the area are long tables and seating influenced by the Prairie School and commissioned artwork which has the feeling of the 1930-ish paintings of Thomas Benton Hart; rich deep colors with an overall earth-tone quality also seen in the WPA paintings of that period.

MARSHALL FIELD'S

Water Tower Place, Chicago, IL

Design: Schafer Associates, Inc., Oakbrook Terrace, IL
Project Planner & Principal in Charge: Robert W. Schafer/
Ronald H. Lubben, F.I.S.P.
Creative Director: Barry Vinyard
Project Manager: Donal Bona, I.S.P.
Photographer: Bob Briskey, Briskey Photography,
Chicago, IL

The Water Tower Place on Chicago's prestigious shopping street, No. Michigan Ave., is by now a well established high rise shopping center and the Marshall Field's store has been a 284,000 sq. ft. anchor for this mall since its inception. To appeal to the diverse customer base and convey "an upbeat, urban spirit and sophisticated look," the store has recently undergone a partial remodel and this, the men's area, has been completely redesigned by the Schafer Associates.

Additional objectives for the remodeling included providing a consistent image and clear circulation pattern, integrating large scale columns into the design, creating a spacious atmosphere in the relatively small floors. Traffic flow was improved by creating clear, direct main aisles "that draw customers through the departments and allow multiple merchandise categories to be viewed simultaneously." Floor and ceiling details in addition to cove lighting along these paths reinforce the traffic patterns and act as points of reference.

With its own entrance, the Store for Men was designed to feel like a specialty store. Low ceilings give the space an intimate, boutique-like ambience. "The focus is on detail at the front line with dominant presentation of merchandise all the way to the back walls."

Men's shoes were, for example, integrated within the suit department thus providing the customers with everything they need to complete an ensemble in one place. It decidedly encourages cross selling. To add some flair to the typically traditional Men's Shirts area, a curvilinear theme was introduced that was carried through in the fixtures, the tables, columns, lamps, ceiling details, and even in the multi-colored, free form, custom designed carpeting.

FREY

Aarau, Germany

Design: Umdasch Shop Concepts, Amstetten, Germany
Architect: Martin Ruch

The Frey men's shop has many branches throughout Germany and the shop's concept has undergone many design changes as it has moved farther away from being a "traditional family" firm with its own lines of merchandise to a more internationally fashion-focused firm carrying brand names and designer apparel like Trussardi, Louis Ferraid and Viventi.

With the change of merchandise there has come a change in merchandising — and store design. This is the newest retail setting created for this well established company by Umdasch Shop-Concepts. "The completely newly designed premises enhances the changed range of articles. In addition, the optical and functional transformation manifests the desired corporate identity. The system-oriented presentation of articles developed by Umdasch also had a positive effect — with respect to costs and work schedules as well."

The gray-white vinyl floors are inlaid with strips of natural, reddish-brown wood and accented with black vinyl squares. The same colored wood is used for the wall system and for the fixtures and cases out on the floor. A "truss" design of black lacquered metal appears as an accent on the glass topped tables, on the stepped shelf floor fixtures and especially on the step ladders that roll around a black rail providing access to the upper shelves. In addition to the black, dish-shaped uplights which are attached to the wooden fins of the wall system, there are MR16s suspended down, on rods, from the black electrical tracks set in the reflective ceiling. Additional recessed fluorescent fixtures, with egg-crate baffles, are set in the ceiling to provide more ambient light.

AXEL

Aarhus, Denmark

Design: Jorn Hansen AS, Kolding, Denmark
Designers: Jorn Hansen & Klaus Nielson

Jorn Hansen AS is a noted Danish store design firm that also creates a variety of unique and exciting wall and floor fixturing systems. When challenged by the owners of Axel to design a special and stimulating store that would appeal to young, affluent men with a taste for better merchandise, they selected their Concorde system to work with. The system is based on both curved and straight modular elements and by combining these modules with new floor units and a special "pyramid" they were able to create a stimulating but still exclusive look in this 2,000 sq. ft. store.

A floor of granite flagstones was laid in a circular pattern near the entrance which is also rounded in sections. The balance of the floor is finished with a light mahogany which contrasts nicely with the modular system. The system is made of stained, bird's-eye maple and trimmed with painted matte surfaces treated to make the surface wear resistant. The fittings are light, nylon treated steel and the shelves are a combination of clear and frosted glass.

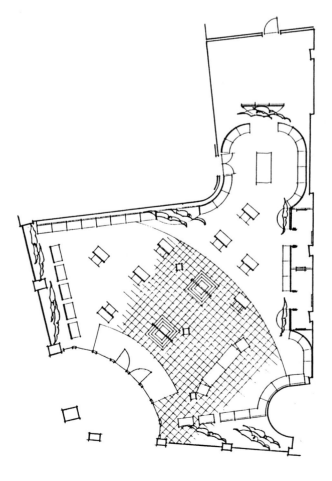

To enhance "an intimate and exclusive" atmosphere, the design firm made use of antique-style furnishings and they also integrated many pieces of artwork into the total design. "Today the store appears as an harmonious and exclusive unit in which the interior style of the store complements the fine branded clothing it offers for sale."

TINO COSMA

Fifth Ave., New York, NY

Design: Rosenberg / Kolb Architects, New York, NY

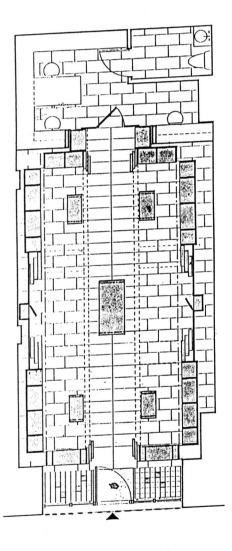

Tino Cosma, an Italian neckwear manufacturer selected a Fifth Ave. store front in the handsome Peninsula Hotel, just off Fifth Ave., to open as his first store in the U.S. Since the "landmark" status of the building dictates specific design guidelines, the forms and materials were somewhat restricted.

The design is simple. The fully-glazed store front "articulates the box and extends clear through the store." The shop front is accented with dark bronze anodized aluminum with gold leaf dimensional signage and custom door handles of pear wood and brass.

Internally, the circulation is defined by the vault down the center of the space and the sales area is delineated by modular custom cabinets that symmetrically surround the space. In keeping with the "simplicity" of the design, the floor is unpolished Beolo granite and the cabinets are made from hardwood pear and pear veneer edged with black metal "C" channels. The modular design concept will facilitate the roll out of fixtures for future stores based on this design. The walls are finished in a mopped, waxed antique stucco finish.

In order to open before Christmas, and with only six months available to design the selling space, draw up the documents, and construct the store, the designers managed to get construction completed in two months at a cost of approximately $500,000 ($500 per sq. ft.). According to the designers of this 1,000 sq. ft. shop "the results are deceptive; a straightforward, modernist design is elaborated by an assembly of rich materials."

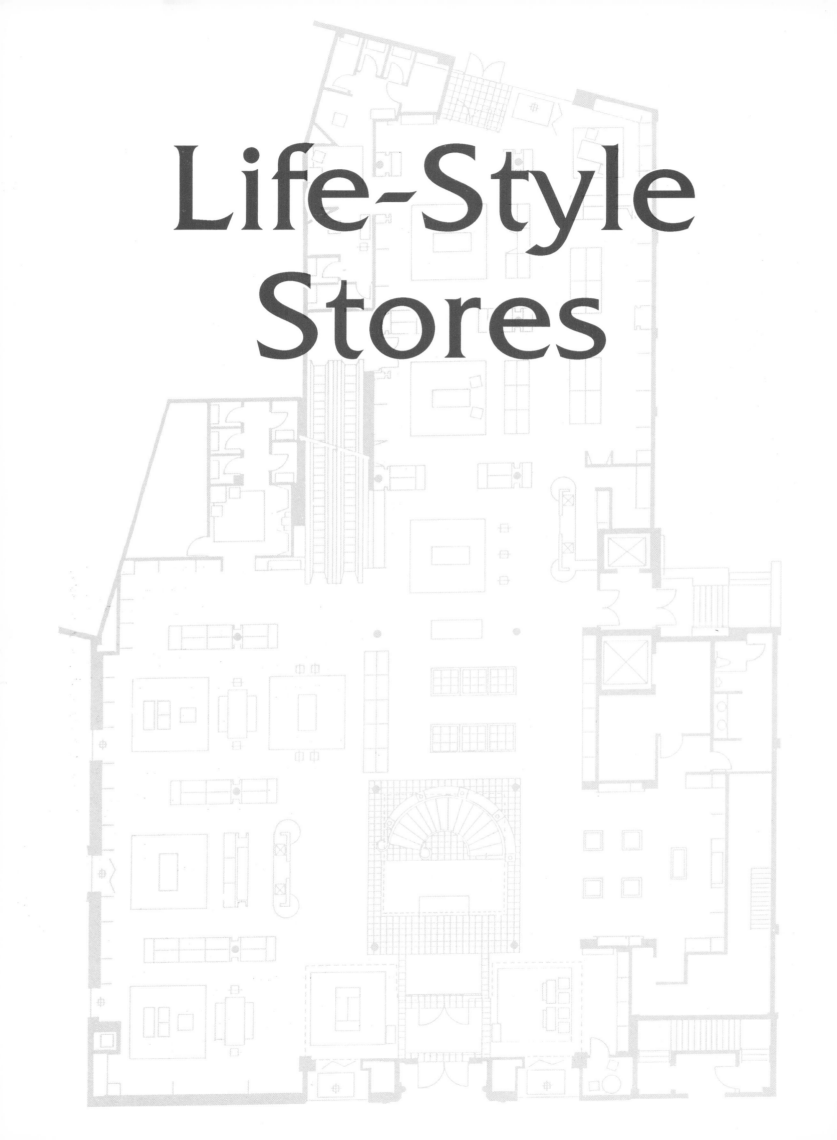

Life-Style
Stores

ALANBY

The Arboretum, Charlotte, NC

Design: Alan Barnhardt & Buddy Hege
Architect: Franklin Buddy Hege, FGH Architects,
   Charlotte, NC
Photographer: John Cress

Alan Barnhardt is not only the owner of the noted Alanby, lifestyle store, his is also the creative vision and excitement that makes the store so unique. The new, two-level store in The Arboretum has 4,000 sq. ft. on the lower retail level and another 2,300 sq. ft. on the upper level.

The architect/design firm that worked so closely with Mr. Barnhardt undertook to create a stimulating retail environment that "would provide opportunity for education while producing a higher level of sales per sq. ft." Hege also had to create the image of a specialty store dealing in outdoor clothing and product on the upper end scale of merchandise; apparel, footwear, and camping equipment that feature brand names like Timberland, Patagonia, Birkenstock, and Sierra Designs.

The materials that were used are for the most part natural. There is high grade wood, stone and other textures and surfaces that match the feeling of the merchandise being sold. An atrium effect was designed in the front entrance so that visitors can look up and see the camping supplies. Since shoppers are usually loath to shop the upper levels, the camping gear, which is usually a destination product, was placed on the upper level but made immediately visible from the entrance. Rising immediately to the right of the entrance is a 20 ft. climbing wall which also helps to bring the visitor's eye up to the second level.

Running down the length of the main level is "The Trail to Adventure" — the main aisle which is covered with Tennessee sandstone. This "trail" winds through

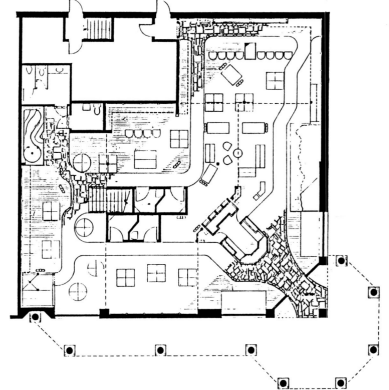

the many merchandising areas on this level which are located on hardwood floors. Also on the entrance floor there is a "waterfall" (sculpted out of concrete and painted to simulate rocks), a rain gear testing storm shower and the persistent sound of cascading water. The paint colors that are used all "represent different elements of nature."

The designers made this store responsible to the human senses "by stimulating those human receptors the visitor will be prompted to interact with his/her environment." Sound and music is integrated into the design so besides the sound of cascading water there are bird and cricket noises in the camping gear area and a variety of music is piped through the store — "reflecting a relaxed atmosphere." To appeal to "touch" there are the stone and hardwood floors underfoot and various surface textures like fabric wall hangings, nylon at the climbing wall, oak fixtures and the rawhide woven snowshoe chairs.

The store is an adventure for all who enter; from those seeking specific merchandise to the kids who can follow animal tracks interspersed throughout the store or visit the Troll's Den which is a vertical, climbing playpen where children can safely play while the parents shop. The hands-on activities, the opportunity to try out the gear as well as try on the apparel in the unique, realistic outdoor atmosphere have already made Alanby's a "must" shop in Charlotte.

JELMOLI

Zurich, Switzerland

The Fitch design group of London started working with Jelmoli two years ago on the complete redesign of the fourth floor of the flagship store in Zurich. The area involved covers 30,000 sq. ft. and is now — in its new design — devoted to lifestyle of the young professional. The finished design — as sampled here — is according to the designers "aimed at young professionals with an emphasis on fashion, audio-visual presentations and sportswear."

Instead of building or laying out traditional departments on the fourth floor, three "worlds" were created; the "world of electronics" with hi-fi/TV, audio media, computers, technical toys, etc. — "the world of Sports" with hardware and fashionable sportswear, and "Spotlight" — the "world of young fashions."

Jelmoli's main desire was to have this as an area where the shoppers can have "fun" — have an "experience." The unconventional plan places accents at crucial points. "A clear special structure helps customers find their orientation and the new way of presenting merchandise in 'worlds' creates additional buying incentives."

Design: Fitch, London
Shopfitting: Vitrashop AG, Birsfelden
Photographer: Phil Ward

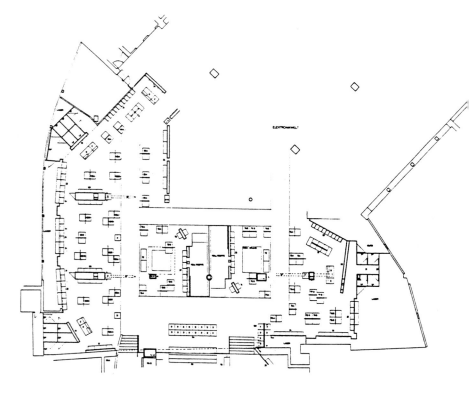

Design Credits:
Design: Fitch, London, England
Design Team: Ken Cosie / Stuart Naysmith /
        Cathy McClymont
Architect: Mr. A. Terazzi

Shopfitting: Vitrashop AG, Birsfelden, Germany
Project Manager: Palf Wolfe
Interior Architect: Harold Schaffer
Dept. Lifestyle Photography: Andrews Heapes
Photography: Phil Ward

In addition to supplying the shelving units, Vitrashop AG of Birsfelden was entrusted with the implementation on the planning concept. They also provided the entire range of merchandise display units. Stabilo wall panels, often used free standing, as room dividers "form the perfect framework for presenting merchandise images as defined by the new concepts of visual merchandising." Louvre screens offer a wide range of presentation surfaces as utilized in the sports footwear area and the Vitrashop's "Vestio" and cross gondolas combined with Ambo presentation tables display the merchandise out on the selling floor with full effect. Fresh and unconventional color and materials — such as unusual combinations of different types of woods — "gives new impulses to shopfitting."

This joint effort by an English design firm and a German shopfitting outfit working together to create a new and exciting lifestyle oriented floor in a Swiss department store is what the Internationalization of Store Design is all about.

SPAZIO

Tokyo, Japan

Design: Interspace Time, Tokyo, Japan
Principal in Charge: Stome Ushidate
Ex. V.P./Int. Design: Hiroyuka Kawano
Exec. V.P./Architecture: Robert Lowe
Design Team: Naomasa Megumi / Chizu Kozo / Hiroyuki
  Yanagimachi / Shinya Harata / Michael Labasan
Photographer: Jun Mitomi

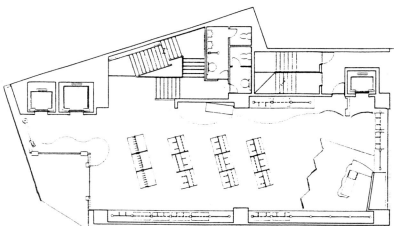

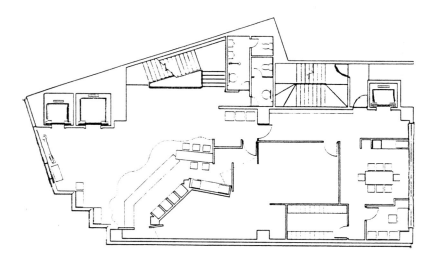

Minami Sports is a large and important sporting goods chain in Tokyo and this, the Spazio store, is located in Kanda — Tokyo's center for sports shops. It is located on a main strip and it is surrounded by the competition. Because of its position, the client wanted this shop to serve as "a landmark — outstanding from others while at the same time be highly flexible in function due to the constant change in season displays."

To complement the nature of the merchandise, the store is designed with a series of bold, whimsical elements and in bright colors. The interior is furnished and finished with an "artistic mixture of terrazzo, wood, and metals." The intent of the design concept is revealed on the store's facade. Designed as a focal point over the entrance is an articulated facade with a variety of strong, architectural features. These are accented with a series of different lighting schemes that also offer an additional complement to what appears inside the store. The lobbies and the elevators to the seven merchandising floors are accented with bright red lacquered wood panels.

The ground level carries a variety of accessories while the succeeding floors are stocked with athletic and sports materials. The customer's service desk is located on the seventh floor. On each level, the counters are the only "functional art" elements incorporated into the spaces since all the furnishings including the merchandise racks and display fixtures are moveable and removable all to provide greater flexibility to the store's layout.

KARSTADT

Munich, Germany

*Design: Vitrashop GmbH, Weil Am Rein, Germany
in cooperation with Karstadt AG's Construction /
Planning / Fitting Dept., Essen, Germany*

"Sport is Lifestyle" — was the caption that was featured when the Karstadt Games & Sports Store reopened in Munich. The Germany department store chain spent much time, energy and money in this "specialized" department store that now covers over 6300 sq. meters (approx. 66,500 sq. ft.). "The house was entirely redesigned and rebuilt — creating a shop with clearly arranged merchandise assortment and well structured presentation."

Everything that makes leisure time fun is now to be found on the four selling floors of this store. The shopper can get expert and comprehensive advice from specialists along with an impressive array of up-graded products.

The ground floor is devoted to sports footwear and gymnastics, while on the first and second floors the shopper can find the equipment and clothes to wear for tennis, riding, fishing, bodybuilding and all sorts of winter sports. They can even find the wherewithal to play such American sports as baseball and football. "The parcellation and the aisle layout were kept to a minimum as the available space was rather narrow.

The new layout lends a 'stadium character' to the shop."

Wooden floors are combined with granite walkways and aisles outlined in black — like an indoor sports court. The palette is made up mostly of neutrals; white, gray, black and natural woods. Bright primary colors are used as accents throughout. Vitraproject, the Vitrashop subsidiary, and Karstadt's own construction/engineering and fitting department jointly handled planning which included the ceiling and light design. The lighting plan combines recessed fluorescents for ambient light and mini-spots for accenting and highlighting. Ansorg supplied and installed the lighting while shopfitting elements were by Vitrashop.

In addition to a toy department on the lower level, there are market stalls on the uppermost level — under the glass dome which hovers over the escalators. Glass elevators also bring shoppers up to this level where they can enjoy assorted gourmet treats. The new store also has an active travel bureau ready to match the holidays to the equipment and clothes purchased in the lifestyle oriented store.

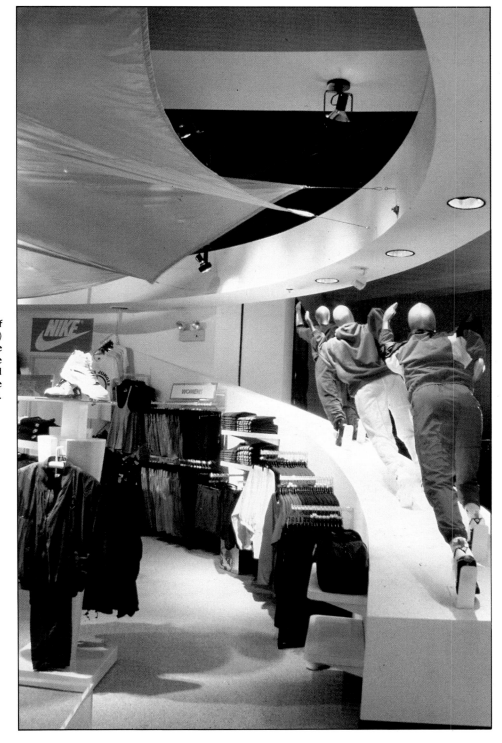

The rising ramp and some of the sail-like canvas fins (right) that appear overhead to create the tent-like ambience. The unfinished ceiling is painted blue and is visible between the circles and the canvas flaps.

A close-up on the giant and the ramp (below) that rises from 2' to 6' with life-size mannequins racing up the incline. Concentric circles pattern the ceiling above.

The non-skid floor (right) resembles a track finished as it is in light and medium gray stone aggregate. Inverted cone-shaped pylons standing just over four feet serve as T-stands. They are topped with 18" circular disks of 3/4" acrylic plastic.

A long view of the selling floor (above) showing the "track" aisle, wall fixturing and shoes presented in sweeping curves on invisible walls; a system of clear acrylic shelving suspended by floor-to-ceiling cables. The modules are laid out to follow the curves of the floor and ceiling patterns.

One of the circular seating platforms that are located on the floor. They are 6'2" in diameter and are either free standing with eight seats or anchored by a conical column with only seven seats as shown here. The seats are topped with day-glow acrylic and the center display is clear glass.

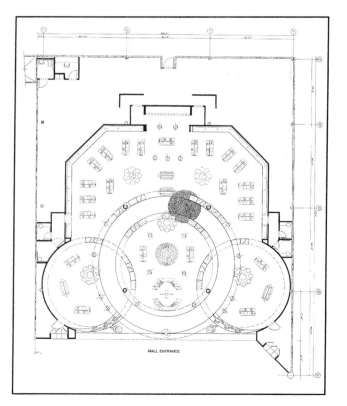

MALL ENTRANCE

KOENIG SPORTS

Millcreek, PA

This prototype store located in Millcreek, PA is a new look for the 79-year-old chain of sports stores. Unlike the previous stores set up by this chain, this new design segments hardgoods from softgoods with an emphasis on ordered display bays. This organization allows shoppers to easily move about and find the specific product categories.

The shopper enters under a large purple disc and then can follow a red perforated metal "wave" which stretches from the disc to an elevated shoe wheel at the far end of the store. This dynamic wave, overhead, is penetrated by some life-size silhouettes of active sports figures. Additional "players" are suspended throughout the space "recalling the motion and energy of various sports."

The hardwood aisle, below the wave, serves to separate hardgoods from softgoods. These areas are further distinguished by the color and material palettes used by the store's designers. The sports fashions are merchandised in warm, neutral and natural materials while the sports equipment is housed in more industrial and hi-tech settings. Both areas are fixtured with a custom unit which allows the product bays to flex with the seasonal merchandise shifts.

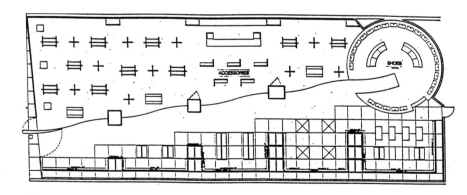

The 13-foot shoe wheel appears at the rear of the store and it is lined with a series of steel poles which in turn support perforated metal shoe shelves. These poles "literally surround the customer — providing maximum product exposure." The recurring circular theme that started with the purple disc up front is repeated through the store and culminates in this focal unit at the far end of the selling floor.

GRAND HYATT WAILEA SUNDRY/LOGO SHOP

Grand Hyatt, Wailea, Maui, HI

Design: AM Partners, Inc., Honolulu, HI
Arch/Design Team: Charles Lau, AIA, President / Jeffrey Kop, AIA / Michelle D'Amico
Photographer: David Franzen, Franzen Photography

Also on the Island of Maui — in Wailea — in another fine tourist hotel is this Sundry/Logo shop which caters to a relaxed and casual lifestyle. The 3,100 sq. ft. retail space is located in the hotel's commercial arcade. What the owners wanted and what the designers, AM Partners, provided was custom designed wall and floor merchandising systems, dramatic lighting, an effective layout, props and accessories that all together enhances the flow of resort shopping.

It is actually two shops in one. In the Logo shop there are areas for resort wear, men's and women's apparel, jewelry and accessories. The Sundry shop is stocked with health and beauty preparations, magazines, books and such. Tying them together is an "elegant resort oriented modern Moroccan theme." Whimsical palm trees are columns and special ceiling treatments and detailed floor patterns are combined with the unique and ornamental casework. A fabric curtained ceiling creates a focus for the shop and the customer circulation follows a convenient path — "to encourage the sales of impulse items."

EQUIPMENT

Madison Ave., New York, NY

Architect: David Chipperfield Arch., London, England in association with Fellows / Martinez, New York, NY
Photographer: MMP / RVC

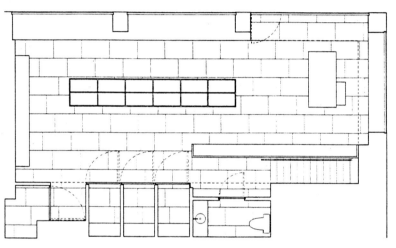

The 1,000 sq. ft. store with windows on two sides has a stark, minimalist, super modern look about it. The store is the New York retail outlet for Equipment SA of Paris and basically the same store houses the company's shirts for women and men.

When this shop was reviewed in *Interior Magazine,* they spoke of Equipment's shops in London and Paris which proclaim "a pared down aesthetic where the folded shirts, in their fine silk and cotton fabrics, dominate the interior from bold, clean line display fixtures." David Chipperfield of London has designed these spaces in Europe and he called upon his fellow architect in New York, William Fellows and his associate Anton Martinez to create this new, clean totally uncluttered and un-detailed interior. The mezzanine that once existed was removed and the entrance door was replaced back to its original corner location. The neutral space has painted walls and a floor laid with pietra serena stone. The three dressing rooms are located behind flush pivot doors on one wall.

Dominating the center of the space and inviting the women shoppers to shop around it is a glass and metal, multi-tiered shelf unit that was created by a sculptor and metal forger. Along the one long wall in the store is a long mahogany unit with shelves and storage space where the men's shirts are neatly folded and stacked. Up front, near the entrance, is the cash/wrap desk which is finished with patined steel.

There are no displays in the window of Equipment. Instead the Madison Ave. shopper is invited to look into the open, clean store beautifully and warmly illuminated by the lamps that run the length of the store. This store was completed in ten weeks at a cost of $265,000 ($265 per sq. ft.).

MARGARET HOWELL

Brooks St., London, England

Design: Caulder Moore Design Consultants, Windsor, Berks, U.K.

The almost totally glazed facade of Margaret Howell shows off the women's wear which is presented on the street level of the shop.

After the success of the first Margaret Howell shop on Beauchamps Place, also designed by Caulder Moore, this second shop was commissioned. It is a two-level selling space of about 1200 sq. ft., and it is located on Brooks St., a small but fashionable street just off Bond St. in London.

The product line — both for women and men — is Classically English; "timeless designs with a slightly retro feeling."

In reviewing this shop, one English fashion publication said, "If it's old, the Brits love it. Longevity is an affirmation of worth, quality and stability" — and the Margaret Howell shop is decidedly 'English' in look — with ecclesiastical, almost monastic, simplicity."

According to Ian Caulder, "We deliberately steered clear of the Mulberry and Ralph Lauren look. The brief was for a low-key but unique and sensitive design synonymous with the Margaret Howell style." There is no propping in the store with "life-style" bric-a-brac.

The designers used natural materials in creating the setting — to enhance the natural fabrics and the neutral palette of the clothes. The floor is laid with dolomitic limestone slabs and an aged oak table is used along with hand made arched frames which all add to the rustic quality of the design which is basically contemporary and simple.

Women's wear is presented on the street level of the shop and a curving staircase leads to the lower level where the menswear is to be found. The lighting is almost all incandescent and the lighting plan includes down lights set into the ceiling, some pendant lighting fixtures and fluorescents hidden behind the fascia to light up the rear wall.

Two views of the lower level. An occasional black supporting column adds a contrast to the neutral/natural setting. The space suggests "permanence — without looking 'designed.'"

URBAN OUTFITTERS

Third St. Promenade, Santa Monica, CA

Design: Pompei AD, New York, NY
Principal in Charge: Ron Pompei
Urban Outfitters: Richard Hayne, President / Susan Ratter, Creative Dir.

The two story, 16,000 sq. ft. store on the southwest corner of the Third St. Promenade in Santa Monica is Urban Outfitters' first venture into southern California. This store, the 14th for the chain, is targeted at the 18-30 year old market and for this the location couldn't be better.

Following the design concepts laid down originally by Richard Hayne, the president of the company, this operation also has a "non chain store" approach to retailing. Richard Hayne said, "Behind our success lies finely tuned merchandising and a signature store environment. We fuse urban energy with a youthful sensibility to make shopping an adventure." Casual clothing is the core of Urban Outfitters' business and it is offered in a wide range of prices and styles for the customer conscious of fashion trends — "but intent on dressing to express himself or herself rather than a fashion ideal."

The industrial building that is now Urban Outfitters was constructed in 1927 and it has now been converted into 8,000 sq. ft. of retail space. The two floors are linked by a monumental staircase of raw steel that descends "through a crater-like opening in the concrete floor." A mid-stair sales platform encourages shoppers to move freely between upper and lower levels. Four layers of drop ceiling were removed to reveal the original 30 ft. high wooden ceiling and skylights. Also, to take advantage of the wide street frontage, the designers gutted the facade and exposed the original structural frame. They then installed gigantic windows to highlight the activity inside the store.

As in the other Urban Outfitters projects, the design firm, Pompei AD, used what they call "selective demolition." The construction crew working under Ron Pompei pealed away layers of existing architecture to reveal glimpses of "urban history" beneath. Rugged steel supports and beams, plaster walls, original brick, a maze of heating and ventilation ducts were revealed. Objects found during the demolition and in scavenging missions are also creatively re-used like the salvaged wooden doors with colored paint flaking that now serve as entrance doors to dressing rooms. On several walls collages have been artistically assembled from scraps of oxidized metal, concrete, brick, broken pottery and aged wood.

"The Urban Outfitters environment can be viewed as layers of time," said Ron Pompei. "We try to investigate and experiment with that idea — to take an approach that's analogous to our client's life experience. Young adults are in the process of self-discovery. They are constantly testing, growing, redefining what's important to them. That kind of evolution over time is reflected in the Urban interior."

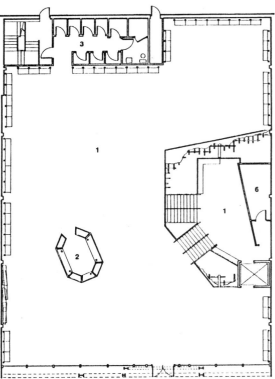

NORTH BEACH LEATHER

The Forum Shops, Las Vegas, NV

Design: Brand + Allen, Houston, TX
John Allen and Howard Hill
No. Beach Leather Design Consultant:
Steven Frank
Photography: Jud Haggard

The facade of North Beach Leather. Note the effective contemporary element of the stainless steel awning frames and the stainless steel signage over the entrance.

The North Beach Leather shops are noted for their colorful, trendsetting clothes and their classically elegant retail settings. It was an easy move for Brand + Allen's design team to move into this space of 2400 sq. ft. with an 800 sq. ft. mezzanine in the Roman-inspired setting. The facade of the store features a series of flattened arches with contemporary stainless steel skeletal frame "awnings" over them and an arced canopy extending out from the recessed entrance into the shop. Since the area in the mall where the store is located required "awnings" — and since the space is an interior one — these awning frames were designed. A frieze of stylized acanthus leaves and acroteria sponged in pale colors runs across the facade over the stainless steel framework.

Inside the store is open, spacious and totally neutral. Creamy white ceramic tiles are laid up front near the entrance under the floating canopy inside the store which has the same shape as the pattern on the floor. Further back a light, natural wood is used on the floor and the wall fixtures are all a pale, warm beige color. Some of the walls and fixtures are finished with a gentle faux finish that is reminiscent of the stone and plaster finishes used in ancient Rome. The main cash desk is faced with a peach colored wood veneer as is the rear partition wall which is arced and hung with face-out garments. Behind that partition are two dressing rooms. The curve of the partition walls complements the "rotunda opera house space" in the middle of the store as well as the bowed end of the floating canopy at the entrance. Stairs behind one of the doors in the rear of the shop lead up to the mezzanine and the balcony that serves as a display stage inside the store. It stars a modern day Romeo and Juliet in coordinated leather outfits.

Another boat-shaped form is dropped from the ceiling at the rear of the store and the floor fixtures also are "boat shaped." Lighting is provided by ceiling washers, downlights, and special MR16 lights bracketed off the walls to highlight the hanger hung garments on the walls.

In creating the central "rotunda" space the designers also created two additional dressing rooms and a storage area.

A view of the shop looking towards the front entrance into the store. Note the floating canopy that gets wider as it approaches the circular selling space in the center of the shop and how the curved end of the canopy is echoed in the floor design where the white tiles give way to the wood flooring. The boat shaped fixtures on the floor repeat the same basic line.

Looking towards the rear of the shop. One of the dressing rooms is up front on the right and the other two are located behind the wood partition wall under the display balcony. The faux stone finishes on the walls and fixtures can be appreciated in this view.

WILSONS LEATHERS

Mall of America, Bloomington, MN

Design/Architect: Shea Architects, Minneapolis, MN
  in cooperation with Wheeler Hildebrandt & Associates,
  Minneapolis, MN
Lighting: Schuller & Shook, Inc., Minneapolis, MN
Photographer: MMP/RVC

Wilson's Leather Shops are familiar to anybody who shops malls across the U.S. For the opening of the Mall of America, Wilson's went all out with this large store — all on the ground level where they could show off not only men's and women's leather coats, jackets and clothing, but a full line of leather accessories as well. This store is, therefore, unique in that it combines two stores in one. There are two major entrances into Wilson's from the mall and one leads directly into the area where the leather accessories are featured and displayed on specially designed fixtures that seem to exclude themselves from the fashion merchandise beyond. Yet they are designed and located to allow the shopper to meander into the area beyond.

The walls are mainly painted off-white and the floors are laid with natural oak wood. At the entrance the floors are paved with off-white ceramic tiles into which the Wilson "W" logo is embedded. Framed and outlined floor fixtures complement the wood framing on the wall units and illuminated panels and the sweeping curves that appear on the walls culminate in the rounded cash/wrap desk that seems to be the hub of the selling floor.

The clean, open space is alive with light. Recessed fluorescent fixtures in the ceiling and the fluorescent tubes hidden behind the coves to light up the ceiling are balanced by the many recessed and swivel incandescent lamps that highlight the merchandise displayed face-out on the walls and on the floor fixtures as well.

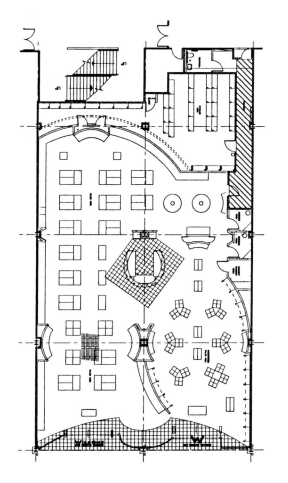

THRIFTY'S

Orchard Park Mall, Kelowna, BC, Canada

Design: Space Design International, Cincinnati, OH

Thrifty's exterior sign is made of aged copper with copper verde accents — to add to the store's "honest, well-worn" image. Here is a look into the store — the main and dividing aisle and the custom gondolas.

Thrifty's is a major Canadian chain selling denim and casual sportswear to a market of young men and women under the age of 30. This prototype store design by Space Design International was created to "make the store easier to shop by organizing the merchandise more effectively and simplifying the layout." Thrifty's also wanted their stores to have "a stronger personality" which would also reflect the company's tradition and heritage as one of Canada's most established retailers.

The 2700 sq. ft. store in the Orchard Park Mall in Kelowna, BC has a simple, symmetrical plan for the long, narrow space. A central aisle divides the store into two; one side for menswear and the other for womenswear. In order to tell distinct merchandising stories, the long side walls are segmented by pilasters and strategically placed gondolas — in the central aisle — which highlight the key merchandise categories. Floor fixtures were designed and located to reinforce the wall displays of garments and the centrally located cash/wrap desk has fitting rooms to either side of it.

"The new store has a deliberately lived-in look — like a favorite pair of jeans that always feels comfortable." This design also complements the casual merchandise on display. To achieve this "lived-in" look the walls are finished in off-white paint to which fish glue has been added. This causes the paint to crack or "craze" and that effect is slightly nostalgic. In the same way "the linoleum tile flooring in the back of the store and the custom-designed gondola fixtures represent updated versions of earlier design elements." The wood flooring is made of maple scraps which shows natural flaws and which also contributes to the desired ambience.

Dressing rooms appear to either side of the centrally located cash/wrap desk. Mirrored doors not only open up the space — they are conveniently located for the shopper's use.

Custom floor fixtures (below are combined with stock racks and the floor fixtures are placed to reinforce the wall

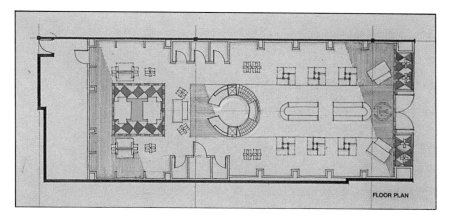

FLOOR PLAN

DOCKERS SHOP

Cambridgeside Galleria, Cambridge, MA

Design: Bergmeyer Associates, Inc., Boston, MA
Planner / Designer: Michael R. Davis, AIA
Project Manager / Job Captain: Rose Narciso
V.P. / Partner in Charge: Joseph P. Nevin, Jr.
For Levi's Only: Tim Sullivan, Dir. of Visual
  Merchandising
Photographer: Lucy Chen Photographer, Cambridge, MA

Most shoppers are accustomed to finding a Docker's Boutique as a shop-within-the-shop of better department and specialty stores. They have proven so successful that Levi's Only Stores, the owners of Dockers, decided to retail the product on their own. To the "more sophisticated than jeans" customer, Dockers offers a more polished, casual wear alternative.

"The objective of the store design was to be honest and straightforward: to develop a store consistent with the Dockers' lifestyle and image, and enhance the product line." The atmosphere is welcoming, friendly and relaxing — "recollective of vacation times and pleasant memories." Also in keeping with the name, a nautical theme was developed that is carried through in the store's design and fixturing.

The traditional storefront plane is set back and the displays are allowed to create favorable impressions with vacation scenes. Angled V-groove, painted panels are stenciled with the Dockers logo "establishing a proprietary, brand-enhancing image." Floor-to-ceiling glass crisply sets off the presentation and cherry wood soffits containing translucent, back-lit, art glass top the display windows. The soffit also frames the arched entry and the floating Dockers sign.

Soft white and warm wood tones appear throughout the store suggesting a summer cottage while the V-groove ceiling soffits trimmed with cherry wood battens recall boat detailing. The beams conceal the track lights that highlight the products casually arranged types of solid cherry tables and three-way fixtures. The perimeter walls are divided into bays alternating free standing and built-in fixtures. Open wood dressers and the shelves that are used are reminiscent of residential furniture. Video monitors appear throughout the space playing classic music videos, Dockers ads, historic newscasts, sporting events, and period commercials.

The cash desk detailing incorporated V-groove panels and signage and the product display at the front is constructed of cherry with a hand rubbed oil finish while nautical detailing is used as an accent. "The Dockers Shop encourages casual browsing in an accessible, unpretentious environment. The design gives broader exposure to the Dockers Line of fabrics, colors, styles and exclusive shirts, with a strong emphasis on merchandise presentation. It fosters individuality and creativity with assurance that the right weekend wardrobe is being assembled."

SILHOUETTE BLUES

Washington, DC

Silhouette Blues as seen from the mall (above). The store is open — totally on view and the displays in the well-lit windows stand out from the store beyond.

Design: Salo Levinas Architectural Design &
Development, Washington, DC
Principal in Charge: Salo Levinas
Project Architect: Joanna Macias
Lighting Consultants: Coventry Lighting &
Steven Greenblatt
Photographer: Maxwell Mackenzie

"Silhouette Blues was created to be a hallmark jean store for the '90s — a showplace of collective memories."

The architects/designers created an innovative space with an exciting design to sell upscale casual sportswear and jeans. "The design was not to be intimidating; it was to be as familiar, functional and inviting to customers as their old pairs of jeans." To answer the clients specific needs and desires, the materials that were used are everyday natural ones like wood, glass and iron — "presented in recognizable forms with simple lines."

The store can be entered both from the street and from the mall — and that created the problem of where to put the service area. The problem was solved by using "imaginative 7'6" plywood partitions that set off angles along the sides of the vanilla colored box." The partitions act as guides for the shoppers — leading them into the selling space while also providing a buffer and thus permitting the perimeter to be used for fitting rooms and storage. The partitions were pre-fabbed and that cut down on the construction time needed on the site.

The service area is partially exposed and the tailor who is there for alterations is on view behind a glass panel.

The decorative details add to the look of the deceptively "plain" space; the galvanized metal lamps resemble headlights off old Chevy pick-up trucks and they light up the merchandise "piled high in stockroom fashion" on the oiled cherry shelves. Shaker chairs are for sitting on and when not in use are decoratively perched on hooks on a wood slat that runs over the garments. The floor is made

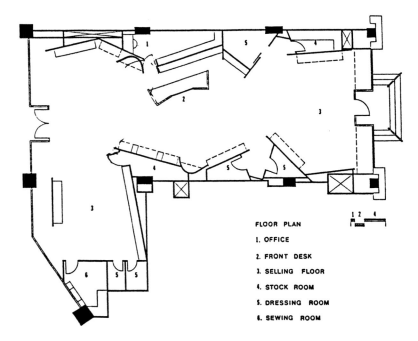

FLOOR PLAN

1. OFFICE
2. FRONT DESK
3. SELLING FLOOR
4. STOCK ROOM
5. DRESSING ROOM
6. SEWING ROOM

up of wide planks — like an old West Saloon. The weathered birch "inner shell" contrasts with the exterior fresco-like walls. "There is no over-design or sleekness."

Silhouette Blues "dismisses unnecessary detail to embrace an unassuming style that puts customers at ease and allows them to concentrate on the merchandise."

The store's design is deceptively simple — un-trimmed or overly detailed and the merchandise stars in the clearly defined and well organized visual merchandising program. The space is woody, warm and user-friendly.

Hanging down over the padded, suede covered counter are the galvanized metal lamps. The wall behind is weathered birch wood which contrasts with the vanilla colored fresco-like walls. The shelves are oiled cherry.

DI FIORI

Morumbi S/C, Sao Paulo, Brazil

Design: A+E Arquitetura
Photographer: Nelson Khon

Di Fiori is the prototype store developed by A+E for a manufacturer of young fashions. The uni-sex boutique specializes in jeans — and the go-with accessories one traditionally wears with jeans.

Honoring the manufacturer's request, there is lots of stock on open display — and the floor standing fixtures, also as requested, is made of wood and stainless steel. The all-important store logo — like a surf board — floats over the selling floors and it is brilliantly illuminated from behind while all around the ceiling is black and patterned with incandescents around the logo-sign. From the mall the shopper sees the Di Fiori sign over the door and the aforementioned floating panel.

The facade (above) as viewed from the mall. In addition to the store's name over the door, the illuminated "surf board" logo panel is also immediately evident.

The right hand side of the shop. The display window is on the right. Note that the dressing room doors and the fascia over them are completely mirrored.

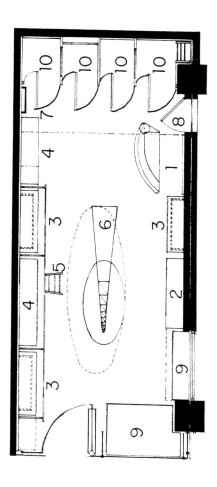

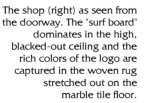

The shop (right) as seen from the doorway. The "surf board" dominates in the high, blacked-out ceiling and the rich colors of the logo are captured in the woven rug stretched out on the marble tile floor.

On the left wall of this long and quite narrow mall space there are dark wood shelves that literally climb up to the black ceiling and a library ladder on a rail which is provided so that the salespersons can get to all the merchandise stocked on the selling floor. The wall opposite has shelves for shirts and sweaters — also of the same dark wood, but they don't go up as high.

The floor is laid with creamy white tiles and a native woven runner in earth tones adds a colorful accent on the floor. A wood and steel table, capped with glass, sits in the middle of the floor. The glass shelf is supported on an angled bracket made up of a web of stainless steel rods.

At the far end of the store there are four dressing rooms and the fascia above them is mirrored so that the illuminated ceiling logo plaque and the artwork over the sweater/shirt shelves are echoed back into the store's design. A curved cash/wrap desk is located near the dressing rooms to facilitate the sale and also it is a good place from which to see the whole store.

Because this is a corner store in the mall, there are windows to the right of the entrance and also at right angles to them.

THE ORIGINAL LEVI'S STORE

Lexington Ave., New York, NY

Design: Bergmeyer Associates, Inc., Boston, MA
Planner / V.P. in Charge: Joseph P. Nevin, Jr.
Designer: Michael R. Davis AIA / Randy Bayer
Job Captain: Jeanne Carey, AIA
Project Manager: Dan Broggi, R.A.
Retailer's Design Team: Tim Sullivan, Dir. of Visual
*   Merchandising / Barbara Kates, Visual Merchandising*
Photographer: Chun Y. Lai, Photographer

In 1990, Levi Strauss and Co., the world's largest apparel manufacturer, developed a program for The Original Levi's Store, a specialty store that would carry a definitive selection of the company's jeans and feature a selection of Levi's shirts, tops and accessories. "The goals of the program were to enhance the Levi's brand in a retail environment and to demonstrate Levi's commitment to customer service." After defining and refining the design concepts, this flagship store was opened on Lexington Ave. in NYC opposite the equally famous Bloomingdales flagship store.

The two-level store has a wide frontage on the heavily trafficked street and has a 20 ft. ceiling and unlimited storefront visibility. The store front design is filled with "repetitive openings with freestanding, slab-like elements, alternately presenting super-graphic images and the familiar Levi's logo." The interior side of each "slab" is a jeans bin unit or a merchandising bay which contributes to the store's product capacity.

The shopper enters the store over floor display cases. Broadly curved feature walls flank the round, tiered table fixture which shows off the newest Levi products. Surrounded by 16 feet of jeans and shirts is a focal area

with nine video monitors playing music videos and Levi's commercials. Overhead, the ceilings were conceived as overlapping rectangular planes at varying heights and 12 ft. ceiling slabs are used to define each of the two cash/wrap counters and the accessory areas adjacent to the main space. There are perimeter wall fixtures of Silver Tab jeans which also incorporate the brand's advertising graphics into the presentation. Mostly jeans walls dominate the perimeter of the store broken up by hanging bays topped with display platforms. The primary selling space is below the nine ft. horizontal line that divides the fixtures.

Cherry stained maple, satin nickel hardware and trim, a red striped rustic maple floor, and the bright, primary Levi's red are the store's major materials and colors. Perimeter track lighting is suspended from a custom support system. Compact fluorescent downlights and wall washers provide the ambient lighting.

"The store has a certain landmark quality, appropriate to a brand as widely recognized and steeped in legend as Levi's. But it also delights in the exuberance of its youthful clientele, and is as dramatically scaled as the city it inhabits."

MUJI

Queen St., Glasgow, Scotland

Architects: Harper Mackay, London, England
Designer: Richard Woolf
Assistants: Peter Fearon Brown & Fiona McDaniel
Photographer: Dennis Gilbert

The Muji "no brands goods" store was founded in 1980 in Japan as a reaction to the Japanese "obsession" with labels. Muji is now Europe's first Japanese micro store chain offering basic but stylish merchandise. The first store for this chain, in England, was created by Harper Mackay in a Victorian warehouse in the Covent Garden section of London. This Glasgow store is the second for Harper Mackay. It is located within Glasgow's "Conservation Area" — a landmark district — and it is part of the imposing Scottish red sandstone guildhall. At about 4,000 sq. ft. of selling space it is the biggest Muji store outside of Japan.

The architects/designers built on the concepts and techniques developed for the London store. Here, too, they make full use of the spacial qualities inherent within the building. "Baronial, load-bearing, sandstone walls — exposed at demolition — have been left complementing the raw, untreated concrete and stone floor." The environment is conducive to "no brands goods" and it creates a "timeless chic suitable for housing the beautifully made but strictly minimalist and functional goods."

The shelving consists of a standard metal system for the household units and Harper Mackay created special floor units made from elm and raw steel sections. A secondary household area — reached by a generous dais and stair configuration displays the full Muji range of furniture, bed linens and kitchenware. The "fashions" or soft goods are shown on the main level on the wood and steel fixtures.

Hanging like a "good luck charm" on the wall is a bicycle. The impact of the design and the engineering of that bicycle on the editors of the Tokyo Creative Catalogue moved them to describe it as, "A bike to hang on your wall as well as ride." It explains somewhat, the concept behind the "art" of the product and the respect for the "honesty" of good materials and construction in the "no brands name" goods.

Lighting within the interior emphasizes the architectural composition of the scheme "with an accent on expressing the high vaulted roof structure and pinpointing the merchandise display at low level." Natural light has been introduced along the side wall by exposing previously blocked-up side windows.

Fashion Accessories

O.J. PERRIN

Ave. Montaigne, Paris, France

Design: Euro RSCG-Agora Sopha, Paris, France
Principal in Charge: Roland de Leu
Project Designer: Frederique Sebaoun

For anyone who has strolled the world renowned Faubourg St. Honore, in Paris, and on the elegant streets that angle off it, the Ave. Montaigne is indisputably "the heart of luxury retail" in Paris. Surrounded by famous fashion designer boutiques and salons is O.J. Perrin. Nicholas Perrin, the reputed jewelry designer, decided to open his store here as an international showcase for his talent. Euro RSCG--Agora Sopha was commissioned to turn the long, narrow space of 45 sq. meters (400 sq. ft.) into a fitting setting.

The design concept was to be modernistic — "with an air of creative insolence" which would stand out from the "classically traditional style" prevalent on this avenue. The high point of the design concept is a tall curved wall which undulates down the central line of the shop. It is made of stone, with an arch and niches which serve as display cases. The stone has been artistically sculpted — with jagged edges and crumbling sides — "creating an image of the past — weathered by the cataclysm of creation." On the two side walls all the fittings for both storage and sale have been grouped discretely into bleached gray wood panelling.

Suspended down from the panelling and bathed in the intimacy of the downlighting are small desk tops made of glass slabs. As another salute to the past, there are Louis XVI chairs covered in bright, strong colors; red, green and yellow. These colors echo the packaging of the products and the sales catalogues.

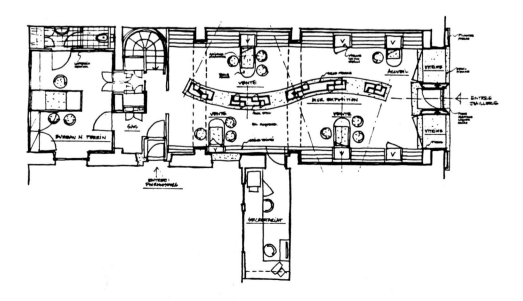

SCHULLIN JEWELRY STORE II

Kohlmarkt, Vienna

Design Firm: Atelier Hollhein
Architects / Designer: Prof. Hans Hollhein
Photography: Gerard Zugmann

In the heart of Vienna's elegant shopping district — just off the world famous Graben is the equally renowned Kohlmarkt which leads to the Imperial Palace. Here is located the second Schullin Jewelry store also designed by Hans Hollhein. The first store, on the Graben, was both architecturally and commercially acclaimed and so a new space needed to be constructed.

The major problem facing the architect/designer was the narrow street exposure of this rather small store which is only 14 meters square. The architect chose to "expose the basic masonry structure of the existing building and restore it to the original appearance, setting in front of it an independent entrance object of wood, bronze and an irritating piece of red fabric." In a "contradictory gesture," Prof. Hollhein "punched through" the bearing pillar to create an entry on a central axis between the two display windows. "Thus the whole concept of an overlay of a symmetrical system with an asymmetrical one — coming back to concepts developed years before on the basis of studies of an aircraft carrier."

On the interior, because of the demands of the existing structure and the way up to the second floor, the continuing path in the store deviates from the axis.

Here, too, the old vault structure of this early 19th century building was "set free" and the space was not conceived as "a second new shell but the new installations were in a dialectic with the old given condition."

The new materials used in the store were wood (briar) and stone (rosso verona) which have similar visual appearances. The stone appears real as well as in an artistic "faux" rendering and as a laminate material. Hans Hollhein says, "Materials, in my work, are not selected for the material, economic value, but for their architectural value. Thus, he uses 24K gold leaf for the reflectors in lamps and combines them with "cheap industrial structured aluminum floor sheets" which are used for the same purpose.

Light is of prime importance in the shop. Here the lighting plan provides a general diffused light ambience, "an atmosphere of serenity," as well as an overlay of many individual point light sources — "their reflection providing the luster of the precious stones."

"The concept of an almost processional path from outside to inside, creating also multiple layers of transparencies, provides varied uses of the different parts of the store — from the more public to the extreme private areas."

LALAOUNIS JEWELRY STORE

Madison Ave., New York, NY

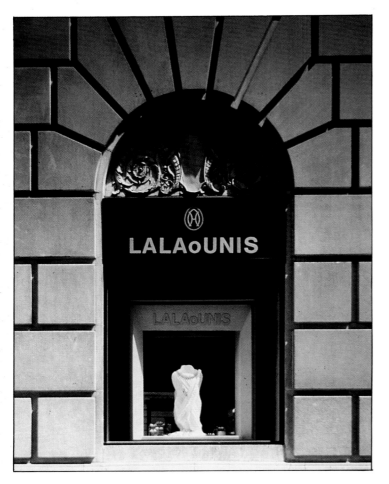

*Design / Architect: Haverson Rockwell Architects P / C,
New York, NY*
Photographer: Paul Warchol

The new 1,500 sq. ft. shop on a prominent corner in the noted upper east side of Manhattan is the showroom and retail store for the world famous jeweler, Ilias Lalaounis. The retail showroom is located on the street level (750 sq. ft.) while the space efficient offices are located either on the mezzanine or below street level (750 sq. ft.).

To establish identity on the street, new custom gold-leaf signage and custom internally lit window display cases were designed which face onto both street frontages. "We decided the simple, internally lit boxes facing the exterior would work best since jewelry stores remove the merchandise from the exterior boxes at night. We designed the box that looked good with or without jewelry," said David Rockwell, one of the principals at Haverson Rockwell, Architects.

Inside the store the focal area is the mottled Pompeiian red display wall which steps back progressively in a sawtooth plan layout to create a dynamic series of display cases. Each of these showcases is also inter-nally lit and the wall that encases them is decoratively painted, waxed and rubbed, in the signature red color of the jeweler. The store designers selected the subtle, muted red color with beige as the color scheme because it also suggested the ancient palace in Crete and the red color is very complimentary to the gold jewelry. "This rich coloration along with the creamy white of the carpeting and the custom bleached maple woods serve to dramatically set off the gold jewelry."

Great care has been given to lighting the store. In addition to the brilliant shadow box illumination, the display wall also conceals indirect fluorescent fixtures which bounce ambient light off the ceiling to create an open, airy feeling for the space and to balance the warm intensity of the incandescent lights. MR16 fixtures are recessed in ceiling pockets and they provide direct lighting to accent the jewelry on display.

"The overall effect of the design is to provide a simple yet visually exciting atmosphere in which to display unusually designed custom jewelry."

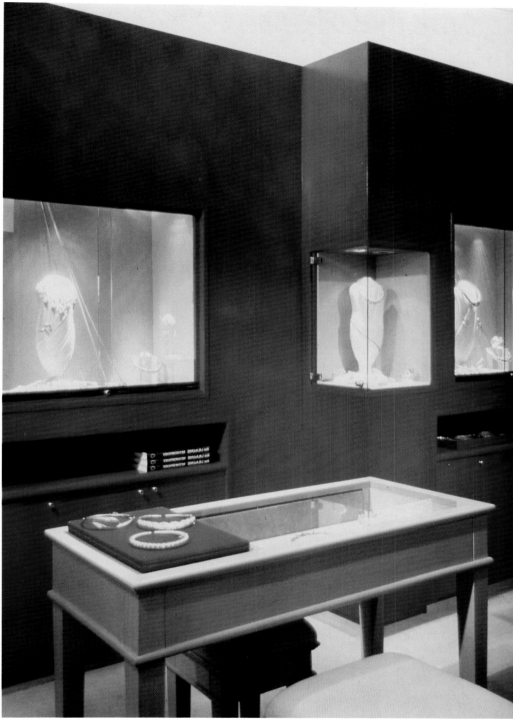

MIKIMOTO

Ginza, Tokyo, Japan

Design: Euro RSCH-Agora Sopha, Paris, France
Principal in Charge: Roland de Leu
Albert Baroka and Ti Komatsu

In planning the refurbishment of their flagship store in Tokyo, the Mikimoto Company, long famous for their cultured pearls and exclusive jewelry, commissioned the Parisian architectural/design firm to redesign the store. The four story building of 18,000 sq. ft. has been divided up as follows: on the ground floor there is a reception area as well as a sales area for high turnover "everyday objects" (engagement and wedding rings) all set out for quick sales to a large, varied customer base. Strung pearls are located on the first level up where there are stand-up counters as well as tables arranged for seated selling. The top of the range merchandise is located on the second level where wholesale selling also takes place. Clients are seated in a "calm, personalized atmosphere." The most expensive range of jewels is on the third and top level of the store. According to the design firm, "here the sales process is treated like a reverent outing. The exhibition is set out on tall curved screens that form separate areas that assure confidentiality and intimacy."

An absolute consistency in style, materials and shapes was maintained throughout. The concept behind the refurbishment was not "to create a sense of hierarchy or discrimination between the clientele — which is both young and ordinary and extremely rich." To accomplish this "consistency" required that the designers consider the functional requirements and the image necessary for the wide range of activity.

The unifying materials used are pear wood, sandblasted or embossed glass, patined bronze and a custom designed carpet whose colors vary from floor to floor. The only elements used to play on the specific character of each floor are the layouts, the merchandising densities and the lighting.

MIGNON FAGET

Lakeside Mall, Metairie, LA

Design: Waggoner & Ball, New Orleans, LA

When the client is Mignon Faget and the jewelry is so classic — so unique — so filled with architectural elements and the wonders of nature — the retail setting does pose a problem. Therefore, as the designers/architects, Waggoner & Ball, stated in their design challenge, it was to create a jewelry store in a shopping mall that "transcends the mundane and mercantile and makes a place distinguishable from the commonplace."

The approach that they took to the design accepted "the given context devoid of natural light and the particularity of the site fundamental to architecture." They employed a controlled but loosely fit collection of forms and elements in subdued shades and placed them within a shell whose walls are overlaid and painted a deep orange sunset color.

The display area finishes include painted poplar millwork and trim, oil rubbed mahogany, painted gypsum board, tempered glass, a sisal rug, slate, and some minimal accents of brushed stainless steel. "The entry portal, the sales kiosk in the center of the space, the wall mounted display cases, the mirrors and the inner room are all designed to stand alone, yet relate to one another as members of a family." These classically inspired forms continue the tradition of New Orleans (just over the bridge) with "obvious reference to its tombs and cemeteries, which also recollect sources as diverse as the Mannerist windows of Michelangelo's Porta Pia and a grove of trees."

"The whole is not a closed set to be experienced in a prescribed way or from particular points of view — but an invitation to the individual to fragment, edit, and recombine as suits his or her instantaneous drive for simplicity or complexity."

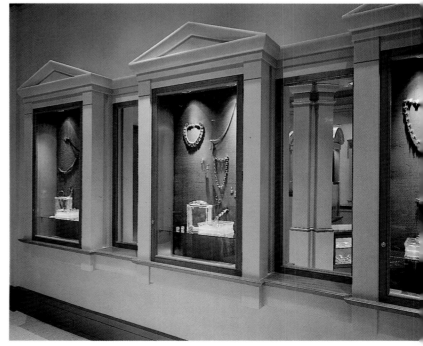

DANIEL SWAROVSKI

Rue Royale, Paris, France

A prestigious Paris address was essential for the first retail store that would be signed Swarovski. The Daniel Swarovski group is famous for its crystal and has also already made great inroads in the fashion world as specialists in "paste" (rhinestones) jewelry. Recently the group developed its own line of up-market products in fashion accessories and crystal giftware and thus this need for a retail outlet.

Though the address was excellent, the designers were faced with some strict limitations: the space is only 270 sq. ft. in size and the store frontage is only nine feet wide. Since there are only a few products in the collection, each item "was of a quality and creative richness rarely seen" so the designers' concept was to create a jewelry store with jewelry display trays. For their design inspiration they took the "Vienna-Paris route." This combines the roots of the company and the creativity emanating from the Cessation of Vienna with the symbols of Parisian classicism.

The overall impression of the small space is of a jewelry box of Louis XVI natural waxed oak panelling divided by large rifts, trompe l'oeil mirrors and black lacquered display cabinets. At the same time, the designers were able to infuse a modern look into the space. "All these factors contribute to creating an astonishing space reminiscent of a theater, and setting the scene for superb collector's pieces by Alain Leger, Ettore Sottsas Mendini and other great artists."

Design: Euro RSCG-Agora Sopha, Paris, France
Principal in Charge: Roland de Leu
Project Designers: Frederique Sebaoun / Andre Thoreau
Consultant: Creative Business, Geneva, Switzerland

S. VINCENT JEWELER

Gaviidae Commons, Minneapolis, MN

Design: Johnson / Reis & Associates, Inc., Minneapolis, MN
Gary L. Johnson, Architect
Photographer: Amathel Sewel

When the 1,000 sq. ft. space on the highly trafficked first level of the shopping center became available, the owner of S. Vincent wanted to relocate from the fourth floor space — and bring the relatively new store fixtures with him. The designer and the owner also decided to make use of some of the things left by the previous tenant; the partial black granite and white marble floor, the recessed halogen lighting in the ceiling and the store front, largely constructed of butt welded glass. "The challenge was to visually adapt and integrate these two palettes."

Mint green and purple anodized aluminum covers were used to clad the neo-classic columns of the existing store front to achieve a more minimalist look — more in keeping with the S. Vincent design attitude. The decorative steel gates which had been designed for the previous location were re-used on the new store front.

Inside the store a curvilinear path of striped green and purple carpet was laid over the existing white marble floor and a new screen wall was designed to conceal the workshop area. The slots between the ash and the African mahogany veneered plywood allow the jewelers to see the customers from the work space. The original display cases were used. They are brushed aluminum jewelry cases resting on black steel bases and they were custom fabricated to look like metal benches.

Three sloped display cases were strategically placed on an interior wall to attract the shoppers in the mall. The panels behind them are off-the-shelf, solid core doors with ash veneer also trimmed with African mahogany.

This is truly a success story in the marriage of "old" and somebody else's "old" to make a refreshingly different "new."

HENRY KAY JEWELERS

Water Tower Place, Chicago, IL

Design: Brand + Allen, Chicago, IL
Project Architects: Robert J. Taczala / Edward Dumont
Photographer: Jud Haggard, Houston

This fine jewelry store is located in the Water Tower Place on the world renowned Michigan Blvd., in Chicago. Though the 1500 sq. ft. space is rectangular, the area is broken up with angled vitrines along two walls and angular cuts through the space to separate the selling floor from the cash/wrap counter, storage and facilities behind.

The shopper enters through double doors placed on an angle (A). The sawtooth arrangement of the vitrines on the interior is first seen from the outside in the honed Dorado sandstone which is used to veneer the two facades of the exterior facing the mall. The display windows appear — on an angle — facing the oncoming traffic on the two major aisles. The staggered vitrines are also of different heights — stepping back and getting taller as they proceed away from the entrance.

The center of the sales space is dominated by a large circular display counter — radiating out around a tall circular vitrine. The cases and the faces of the vitrines in the store are veneered with fiddleback anegre. Stainless steel molding strips and hardware are used to accentuate the casegoods. Metal frames also define the display areas in the wood faced show cases. A round supporting column, up front near the entrance, is now sheathed in stainless steel — providing mirror-like reflections and sparkle. Behind the two wall cases (C) which are equipped with two way mirror panels, is cash/wrap, the vault and storage space. The "Diamond Room" is secluded way off by itself — farthest from the entrance.

As can be seen from the floor plan, the inside layout is 15 degrees off center in order to extend sightlines and "create tension with the perimeter walls."

YAMRON JEWELERS

Waterside Shops at Pelican Bay, Naples, FL

Design: Brand + Allen, Houston, TX
Project Architects: Robert J. Taczala / Gonzalo Olano
Photographer: Jud Haggard, Houston

The Tiffany boutique is located just to the left of the entrance. One of the granite and stainless towers is viewed on the left while another museum case with a granite base stands in the middle of the aisle. The curved counter/case on the right marks the beginning of the Watch boutique.

The 1250 sq. ft. jewelry store was conceived as six boutiques surrounding an entry. Each specialized area or brand name boutique is visually identified by any of the following architectural details; the ceiling may be raised or lowered over the specific area — there may be a special lighting fixture or chandelier located over the space — or it is affected by the relationship between the backwall units and the floorcases. To reinforce the "boutique concept" granite and stainless steel towers were designed and highlighted as accent marks between "shops." These towers are faced with flamed and polished Caledonia granite at their bases and glass cubes are set on top for the display of the precious products. Each tower is capped with a pyramid shaped roof of stainless steel supported on stainless supports set into the bases. Fiddleback anegre wood is used for the floor fixtures, counters and the wall casegoods.

The entry into the shop is set at an angle with vitrine display cases to either side of the entrance. Directly in front is the watch "department" which is accented by a series of arced floor counters that visually tend to sweep the shopper into the body of the space. To the left of the entrance is a small Tiffany boutique. The rectangular display cases/counters with chamfered corners are the designer cases and they are finished with a fine wood veneer plus plinths of the gray granite. The sawtooth arrangement of these are additional "shops": Gold Jewelry, Precious Stone Jewelry, and Semi-Precious Jewelry. A granite and stainless steel tower stands before each of these boutiques and the rear walls are interrupted by display vitrines.

The Watch display area sweeps around the space just in front of the entrance into the shop. Behind the curved wall is the watch repair shop and storage.

The floor-to-ceiling display window is on the far right and the four wood and granite vitrines serve to screen the shop from the street while still allowing "peeks" into the selling space.

The floor of the main body of the store is covered with a rich but subdued shade of plum carpet and the same regal color is used for the fabric lining the stainless steel framed vitrines around the store. In the three rear boutiques and in the area between the front glass windows and the sawtoothed arrangement of counters, the floor is laid in parquet wood. The four vitrines (D) are faced with wood on the inside of the shop and the granite backing is viewed from the outside.

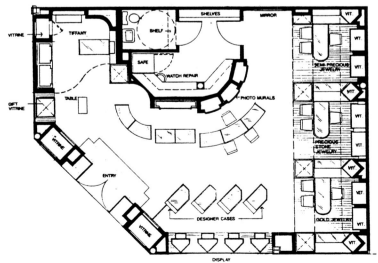

TOM WING AND SONS

Grant St., San Francisco, CA

Design: Brand + Allen, San Francisco, CA
Architects: Chris Harrelson / Eric Brand
Photographer: Jud Haggard, Houston

The facade of Tom Wing and Sons "carries out the Harmony theme in the vibrant city of San Francisco." Chinese red lacquer is the main accent color on the front which is a combination of marble and gold leaf.

The space is small — only 600 sq. ft. — but it is long and narrow. How narrow is obvious from the facade out front which is built between the decorative pilasters of the building. The soft, undulating form of the awnings — the handles on the door and the stylized wave motif on the gold leafed fascia above carry out the "Harmony" theme of the design. The sweeping and scooped awnings are covered with Donghia Regatta fabric and the facade is finished with Italian creme marfil marble. In keeping with the tradition and dictates of the Chinese clients — the facade design is a harmonious juxtapositioning of arcs, curves, and simple rectangular forms.

Inside the small space actually appears larger than it is. The color palette is light and neutral and the casegoods are veneered in sycamore. "The combination of hand picked sycamore with the internally lighted cases provide a unique setting and background for fine jade and pearly jewelry." The floor is carpeted in a muted soft beige and the exposed wall surfaces are painted pale

vanilla. Throughout low voltage lighting enhances the reflective and radiant characteristics of the displayed jewelry.

The fixtures are lined up on either side of a central aisle with a single bowed counter, taller than those to either side, breaking up the straight line of the design. On the left (B) are the lower counters for selling with soft and commodious chairs provided for the patrons. The wall behind has several shadow box displays and a three-shelf wall cabinet, faced with sycamore, complements the arced counter in front of it. On the right hand wall (C) — a counter projects forward to show off more of the displayed jewelry and the rest of the wall is divided in a Chinese key pattern of stepped shelves. The rear end of the shop is staggered — in cubes — thus cutting the long look of the space and the series of rectangular layers that make up the ceiling design repeat the stepped back pattern of the rear end of the space. Beyond the door are offices and storage space.

A view of the shop as seen from the entrance. The single bow fronted counter breaks up the rectilinear look of the shop and it repeats the curves that appear in the facade design. Even the arm chairs pick up the arc motif on their backs.

The right hand wall of the shop is almost all display. Besides being internally lit — a series of low voltage lamps by Ingo Maurer hang from the ceiling to enhance the jewelry presented on the stepped shelves. Note how the lamps created a scalloped — arced pattern — on the wall — in "harmony" with the facade design.

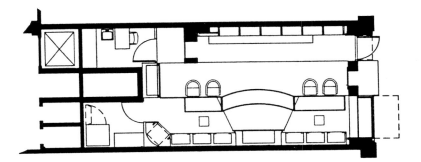

LIZ CLAIBORNE ACCESSORIES

Boca Raton Center, Boca Raton, FL

Design: Brand + Allen, Houston, TX
Project Architect: John Allen, Gonzalo Olano
Photographer: Jud Haggard Photographer

The entrance into Liz Claiborne Accessories. Note that the shoe window on the right is smaller than the bag and sports shoe display on the left. The wood vaulted ceiling can be seen over the central aisle of the shop.

A view of the shoe salon with the four floor-to-ceiling columns and the floor fixtures of bleached oak and stainless steel. Belts are shown on the rear wall and also on the belt fixture standing on the floor. A beige carpet is laid over the bleached oak floor.

The 2300 sq. ft. space in the Boca Raton Center was designed by the Houston branch of Brand + Allen as a prototype store for Liz Claiborne. It is the first store with no ready-to-wear, but is especially designed to show off and sell the Liz Claiborne accessories: shoes, bags, scarves, belts, jewelry and fragrances. According to the architects, "Conceptually — a very well-organized classic statement of wall displays and floor fixturing."

The facade is simple: a wood veneered front with the raised sign over the door illuminated from behind. The entrance is slightly off-center and that puts the whole almost symmetrical floor plan a-kilter with more aisle space on the left hand side. The spacial organization of the floor is accomplished by the use of four full-height display columns which anchor the central core of the space and departments work off all four sides. The columns start with bleached oak bases and matching tops with stainless steel bands and supports.

Glass shelves are supported on the stainless steel vertical uprights and incandescent lamps — embedded in the wood top — allow the light to pass through the glass shelves illuminating the displayed accessories. The central core of the shop is mainly devoted to shoe display and red leather back-to-back couches plus some chairs are located in this beige carpeted area.

Merchandise is displayed on the three perimeter walls which feature arched prosceniums in front of the Zolatone painted walls which are usually furnished with glass shelves. Additional free standing floor units of either bleached oak or stainless steel — or a combination of the two are set about on the floor of the shop.

Suspended over the front part of the central aisle is a partial vault of bleached oak pierced with spots while globe lighting fixtures hang over the shoe area.

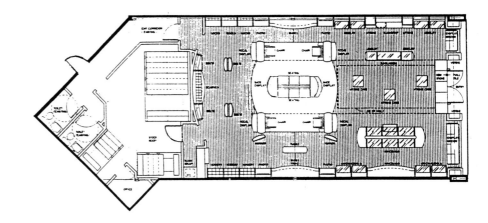

A view of the side wall merchandise displays with the arced soffit or proscenium in front of the painted and glass shelved wall which is fully illuminated by lamps hidden behind the shaped valance. The back-to-back red couches are set in the center of the floor.

COLE-HAAN

Newbury St., Boston, MA

Design: Forbes Associates, Falmouth, ME
Barton A. Forbes
Architectural Consultant: Shea Architects,
Minneapolis, MN

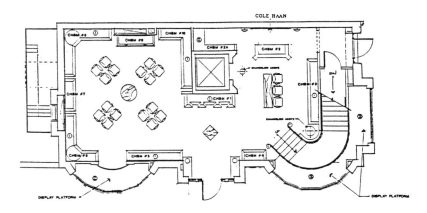

With a 100 ft. linear frontage on Newbury St. in classic, world famous Boston, and in 7,000 sq. ft. set out on three selling floors, the new Cole-Haan store opened. In addition to carrying the famous shoes and leather goods for men, women and children, the store stocks assorted accessories and hosiery.

The facade of the 1870 building was completely restored to its former elegance and classic grandeur while the interior was refurbished as the graceful townhouse it was more than a century ago. "It is a major restoration that both evokes the past and represents the best of contemporary style."

Since this is Cole-Haan's first entry into the Boston market as a retail store, they wanted to generate some excitement about "the exceptional quality we represent and demonstrate in a very visual way the remarkable store it is." Based on an early photograph of the building, the architects were able to "restore" much of the structure's original architectural fenestration of leaded glass windows. The interior was completely gutted but a partial staircase balustrade decorated with leaf carvings that was presumably left from the original design, was located and it served as the inspiration for the new interior scheme. Today, a new/old grand staircase with the same leaf pattern carved on the balusters is the focal point of the interior and it connects the main floor with the first level. Throughout the store the ceilings are treated with plaster molding details and some of these are also enriched with the leaf pattern.

In a past issue we did present another Cole-Haan shop — the one in Florence. According to Michael Carr of Forbes Associates, "Every single job is designed with its own motif and is customized to site." Thus each Cole-Haan store is quite different and special and original. "Our customer is buying a beautiful product and we don't feel that concept would work as well inside a typical store. The architecture should be as well thought out as the product," said Cathy Taylor, Exec. V.P. for Cole-Haan.

This store has won many awards including one from the Boston Preservation Alliance for its "sensitive restoration" of this historic building.

ENZO ANGIOLINI

Willowbrook Mall, Wayne, NJ

Design: Nine West In-House Design Team
James Spodnik, Design
Stacy Lastrina, Director of Visual Marketing
Architect: New Interiors

Long well known and well established in better malls across the country, the Nine West Group now introduces a new line — Enzo Angiolini — with its own distinctive look and ambience.

Working within a mall space of about 1,000 sq. ft., the designers took their inspiration from a quote by Coco Chanel — "Luxury must be comfortable, otherwise, it is not luxury." To interpret that they drew on the sleek and elegant look of the Normandie which reigned as the Queen of the seas during the Art Deco 1930s. It seemed to be the approach to get the look that would complement this collection of fine leather footwear which retails from $60 to $120. The company felt that this new line is an "extension of the luxurious feeling that is synonymous with the Enzo Angiolini name."

The store features a sable mahogany storefront and casework inside along with horsehair-like fabric seating. Combined with a bleached oak floor with sisal insets, these design elements "create a surreal environment, one that entertains and entices the customer with sheer luxury."

NINE WEST

Willowbrook Mall, Wayne, NJ

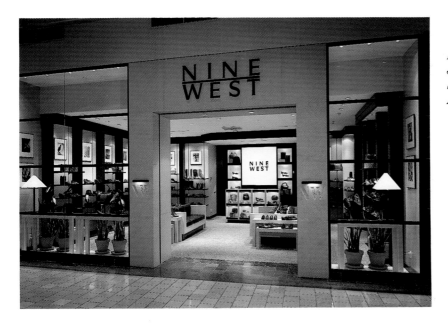

Design: Nine West In-House Design Team
James Spodnik, Director of Design
Stacy Lastrina, Dir. of Visual Marketing
Architect: New Interiors

For many years, shoppers to upscale malls have been greeted by the cool, contemporary, white marble and black trimmed interiors of the New West shoe stores. The company, with this prototype, introduces a softer, warmer design with an etched limestone facade that they feel "reflects the simple sophisticated look that will inspire the customers of the '90s."

To get that new image across, the designers have created cabinetry and wall units of maple wood which are further "warmed" by the use of leather upholstery. In order to affect a more residential look which would more truly showcase the Nine West line, the interior display of shoes is set out on parson tables while black and white photo blow-ups also add to the setting without detracting from the merchandise.

The company believes that this new prototype — "the fusion of modern design elements with the suberb collection" will once again — for the '90s — set this retailer apart from the others in the mall.

SHOOOZ

The Forum Shops, Las Vegas, NV

Design: Colours, Inc., Las Vegas, NV
Architect: Carpenter Sellers Assoc.
Photographer: Greg Cava, Cava Photography,
Las Vegas, NV

"And the earth shook." The earthquake may have cracked marble and splintered glass but here at the Forum Shops, Shoooz stands out as something very old where all around it are new/old designs.

A view of the store's interior with the stone step displayer up front and the curved colonnade in the back of the space. Shoes are displayed on classic wall shelving units which are also finished to look like stone.

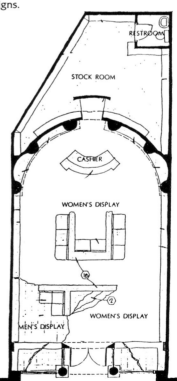

Sal Carsello, the owner of Bianca of Nevada, wanted to offer a complete line of women's shoes including — but not limited to couture. He realized that he needed an all-encompassing price range since the women's apparel stores in The Forum Shops includes Escada and Bernini Donna as well as The Limited.

The shopper's attention is immediately captured, out front, by the "cracked" windows and the shattered facade above it — as though we were in a time warp — back in Pompeii when the earth shifted and quaked. The classic pink "marble" entrance way of columns supporting a lintel remains untouched by the shift and the quake. The store's name ablaze with light shines out into the mall.

Inside the store's fresco painted walls, the classic semi-circular arcade interspersed with arched opening, the "broken" floor of "mosaic artwork" and "stone" all further the imagery of an antique world. The textured "stone" displayer of many steps — up front and center — adds still another "ancient" touch to the interior design. The same rough texture is also picked up in the constructions that line the sides of the shop. The ceiling is washed with a cool blue light to suggest a sky while sports are dropped from the ceiling to light up the shoes displayed on the wall fixtures and the floor unit. At the far end of the shop, a single arched opening leads to the stock area while arched alcoves to either side hold a shelved display of

handbags. The curved cash/wrap desk opposes the curve of the arcade behind it and it is also "textured" and treated to look like stone. The pink/peach faux marble columns in the arcade repeat the motif introduced in the facade's design as well as the logo over the central arch repeating the signage out front.

The cash/wrap desk, the entrance to the storage area and the handbag display in the store. The ceiling is cooly lighted to resemble a summery sky and the sitting area — for trying on the shoes — is just viewed in the foreground.

HOSIERY BOUTIQUE

Ludwig Beck, Munich, Germany

Design: Mathias Thoerner, Munich & New York, NY
Photographer: Beck's Dept. Store

The new 2,500 sq. ft. hosiery department in the noted, upscaled, flagship Ludwig Beck department store in Munich was developed as a prototype concept to be used in other Beck stores in Germany. The hosiery boutique has historically been a very important area in this store's operation and the new design created by Mathias Thoerner has been developed to adapt to larger and smaller hosiery spaces in the other stores. "The custom designed fixtures house the very small and graphically diverse packages within a strong frame, thus projecting a definite image."

Reconstituted wood veneer and black linoleum are the "contemporary" materials used, yet the accents such as the pulls and the tags "are more traditional and transmit a sense of familiarity and accessibility." To add the flexibility required to the design of the space, the walls are painted neutral gray and there is a wire mesh ceiling. The continuous wood floor and moveable, free standing units also add to the flexibility and adaptability of the concept. Though there is a limited range of merchandise, focal displays do maintain the shopper's interest. The design firm was also responsible for the architectural graphic directories and the interchangeable product information panels located on the columns.

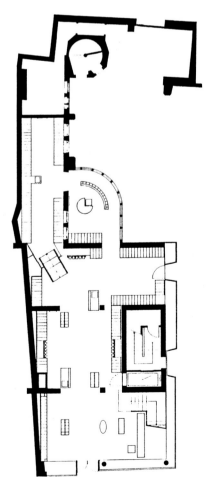

COLAIZZO OPTICIANS

Seattle, WA

Architect: Designer: GGLO, Seattle, WA

The 700 sq. ft. space has been recreated into a combination gallery and laboratory for eyeglass frames and prescriptions. What was previously a dark and depressing space has been converted through the magic of GGLO, of Seattle, into exciting spaces.

It all starts out on the street with the new store front design. The tall, mullioned display window and the window panelled door brings streams of southern light into the deep interior during the daylight hours. Aiding and abetting are the many focusable spots that are lined up on the ceiling and run the length of the store. A giant red neon "O" — superimposed with the name of the store — dominates the facade. Within the store, the designers recall the "O" or circle motif along with other geometric shapes like squares and triangles that are supposed to suggest the eyeglass frames.

Leading from the door is a striking black and white tiled path that accentuates the "gallery" area of the

floor layout. It continues through to the rear of the space past the display of eyeglass frames mounted off lucite bars attached to the white walls. On the other side of the store, on a neutral area laid with industrial-type carpeting is the sales area along with the "private" spaces; laboratory, office, and bathroom.

Throughout the space is dominated by a contrasting palette of red, black and white which reinforces the inexpensive finishes of the paint, laminates, vinyl composition type and industrial carpeting. By working within the owner's extremely tight budget and schedule and by selecting the inexpensive and easily available materials, the designers were able to open the store only seven weeks after the initial design meeting.

According to the judges who selected this store for the AIA/DJC Project of the Month; "It shows what can be done with ingenuity, a low budget and a difficult space."

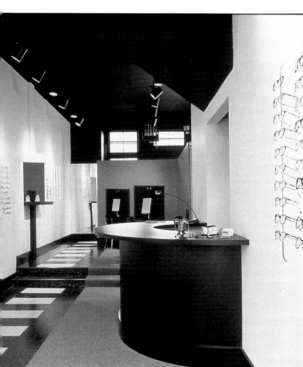

ARTHUR HAYES OPTOMETRISTS

East Grinstead, U.K.

Design: Fitch, London
Design Team: Graeme Elder, Design Director
Christian Davies, Project Designer
Project Architect: Peter Maby, PPI Consultants
Photography: Bruce Hemming

Arthur Hayes Optometrists is an independent chain of opticians in the south of England and "offers high quality service and a friendly, helpful approach." Fitch of London was brought in because the company felt that its current environments did not truly communicate its values as well as they should.

In the East Grinstead store, illustrated here, the space is located at ground level in a 16th century, listed building and in order to get the desired 675 sq. ft., the store had to spread out into the adjacent building. Not only did the store have to read as a "coherent whole," the design firm had to work around "protected columns and beams" in the landmarked structure.

Fitch solved the problem of movement through the space by creating four separate yet connected areas: reception, merchandise presentation, waiting room and consulting and dispensing area. "Colours and finishes are used to filter people from area to area, limiting transitional or 'dead' space." The reception/merchandise presentation area is bright, open and inviting. This is where the bulk of the store's stock is visible and the products are grouped into units according to style and target market. The waiting room beyond is warmer and more relaxed and there is also a provision here for pre-screening. "Specialist light fittings offer a diffused light which contrasts with the directional lighting of the retail area." A spun glass, central ceiling fixture adds to the softened ambience which is enhanced by large upholstered tub chairs — "continuing the theme of a comfortable, relaxing space. The specialist lighting throughout explores optical themes using cast glass lenses to create pools of light around the space." Opaque glass and metal diffusers also help to differentiate the various areas.

The ambient light and the quarry tile floor manage to enrich the functional, consulting room and dispensing area. A custom desk and work station with softened lines also helps as do the warm colors, recalling the waiting room, which allows for a friendly and relaxed interchange between staff and customer.

A new graphic identity was developed with a handwritten "signature" mark and specially commissioned illustrations. This appears on the outer windows of the remodelled store front which unifies the two buildings. A new red oak door with custom ironwork and framed vision panels serves as the new entrance into the shop.

Children
&
The Young
At Heart

MOTHERCARE

Watford, England

Giant, friendly animals stand, up front, before the wide opening into the new Mothercare store. The elliptical sign is supported by "wrought iron" brackets that reach over and across the opening.

The noted U.K. Mothercare store — a division of Storehouse — commissioned the Fitzpatrick Design Group to "create an extraordinary new children's/mother's shop." The requirements were that the store be interactive for children, organized and friendly for easy shopping — especially for pregnant women and mothers with strollers. The merchandise had to be well presented and the space had to be informative and entertaining for the mothers and the children.

Taking their inspiration from the Central Park Zoo in New York City, the designers took off on a park/zoo theme. To create some interaction with the children there are two talking trees; one talks on ecology and the other on safety. As well as evolving a park/zoo look, all the materials selected for the project had to be durable, safe, and non-toxic.

The carpet simulates the green grass scattered with wild flowers while the walkway or main aisle is covered with a stone/pebble textured material. Decorative sign posts add to the out-of-door atmosphere and they also carry the clear, yet playful, signage. The wainscoting was used to further reinforce the park's theme. In the rear of the store there is a "pond" guarded over by a Mother Swan.

The trip from the front entrance to the pond near the rear is filled with fun and adventure for the children as they meet familiar animal friends and the talking trees.

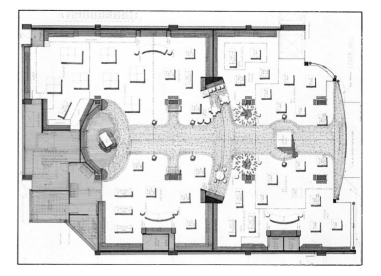

Design: Fitzpatrick Design Group, New York, NY
Design Team: Jay Fitzpatrick, Pres. & Creative Director
Andrew McQuilkin, Designer
Lisa Benson, Dir. of Colors & Materials

The nursery at the very far end of the store. Swans swim about under the raised cupola which is painted to look like a summer sky with some puffy clouds.

A view of the nursery entrance. Note the play area set up on the pebbled stone path where the children can amuse themselves while the mothers shop the area.

One of the talking trees is seen on the far right and the toadstools are just the right height for children to sit on while they "interact".

SO FUN!

Philadelphia, PA

Architect / Designer: The Office of Charles King, P.C., Philadelphia, PA
Principal in Charge: Charles King
Team Leader: Robert Bernstein
Photographer: Thaddeus Gowan, Jr.

"The design challenge was to provide a hip, cool, kid's clothing store using natural materials, primary colors, a neutral background — with a playful, understated ambience." In addition, the design firm was constrained by a small budget — and only a two week construction period!

To creat So Fun!, the design team created an overall ambience of green plywood trees and glowing white clouds. These design elements under a ceiling of stock fluorescent fixtures gave "rhythm" to the long, narrow store. In keeping with the "look," the fitting rooms and the back counter are designed as little houses with brightly colored roofs. In another little house on the floor there is a TV monitor which serves to entertain the kids who couldn't care less while mom and dad shop the store. For economy as well as effect, custom broom head mannequins are used throughout for the display of clothes ensembles — "making it easy to select items from the merchandise which is housed against the walls in stock, natural wood shelving. For the merchandise on the floor, slat-sided crates which support custom designed rods for hanging clothes were selected by the designers. To complete the ambience of the "little town" setting, picket fence end panels enhance the playful, play-town character of the store.

By careful advance planning and preparation of the elements needed for the space, the design firm was able to bring about the metamorphosis of the space in the alotted two weeks.

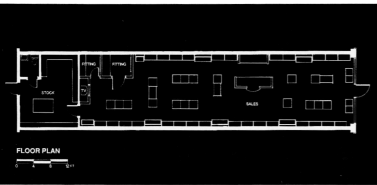

FLOOR PLAN

0   4   8   12 FT

KIDS KASTLE

The Forum Shops, Las Vegas, NV

Design: Colours, Inc., Las Vegas, NV

The entrance to Kids Kastle cleverly integrates the medieval theme and motifs with the "classic" setting. The etched glass is supposed to be the masonry wall of the castle.

Caught in a time warp is Merlin stepping out of Medieval times to preside over the goings on in Kids Kastle which is itself captured and enclosed in the Forum Shops.

Using a less than "classic" approach to the entrance design, the stepped and crenelated design of the entranceway suggests a medieval castle and the dimensional Merlin steps forward to greet the kids in the mall. Since the 20' papier mache dragon that floats through the store is so important, the facade is mainly composed of giant sheets of glass which have been etched with the pattern of stonework. The windows become transparent walls that let the shoppers see into the store.

From the decorative "stone" patterned floor to the castle enclosure that runs around the perimeter walls — all trompe l'oeil artwork and textured "masonry" it is a kid's fantasy come true.

The harmless and almost lovable dragon soars through the blacked out space, above, along with some fluffy cut-out clouds — all in the carefully illuminated void. The children (with their parents) enter the castle through the latticed "portcullis" doors — across the "moat" and onto

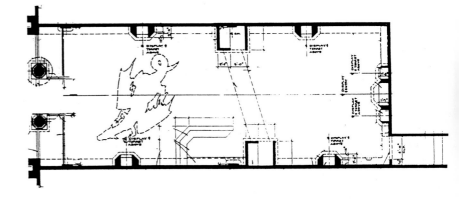

the selling floor filled with children's clothes, some of which are worn by wooden cut-out figures with hinged appendages. In the toy section in the rear of the store, princess costumes, knightly armour, crowns and Merlin memorabilia are offered. Shields hang off the gray stone walls to add some color — and medieval flavor.

The selling floor as seen after entering over the moat. Dominating the upper space is the benevolent 20' papier mache dragon. A castle courtyard is emulated with the "stonework" around the perimeter walls and the simulated "stone" floor.

THE EAGLE'S EYE KIDS

Pigeon Forge, TN

Design: Walker Group / CNI, New York, NY

The prototype store in Pigeon Forge, TN was developed by the Walker Group/CNI for The Eagle's Eye, a company which manufactures high quality women's sweaters. To introduce their special new line of children's sweaters — mainly "novelty" sweaters — the design firm provided this scheme which can be adapted to roll outs around the country. The prototype combines the store's ambient concept and the fixturing required to properly merchandise the stock.

Since the sweaters will be novelty items and usually sell for special holidays or events like Halloween, Thanksgiving, Christmas, etc., The Eagle's Eye Kids store was conceived to have a special events area within the store that would attract both children and parents. It would create the right atmosphere for the sweaters and accessories developed for the children's line.

The color scheme and the materials used are all neutral and natural; a greige colored carpet with light, natural oak floor fixtures accented and topped with white laminates. The walls of this 2,000 sq. ft. store are finished in a pale, warm beige that blends with the wood units on the floor and the generous cash/wrap desk. Rising up in the center of the space is a black "antenna" that rotates. At one end is a model plane that seems to fly over the space and at the other end are cutouts of the moon and stars.

Depending upon the holiday or event — the suspended objects change. An especially fun area, for kids, is the Barber Shop where children can sit in "grown up barber chairs" scaled down to be just right for them. They can be amused by the cartoons that appear on the big TV monitor while the hair cutting experience is going on.

Baffled fluorescent fixtures are recessed into the ceiling and incandescent spots are used to accentuate the merchandise displays. A row of white glass shaded drop lights not only light up the top of the cash/wrap counter, they also emphasize the location of the counter in the space.

LEE'S KIDS

J.C. Penney, Eastland Mall, Columbus, OH

Design: Fitch, Inc., Worthington, OH
Project Manager: Jaimie Alexander
Design Team: Kelly Mooney / Paul Westrick /
*   Maribeth Gatchalian / Paul Lechleiter*
Photographer: Mark Steele

In Books 7 of Stores of the Year, we included some vendor shops and this Lee's Kids, set up in the J.C. Penney store in the Eastland Mall in Columbus, OH is another example of the inroads being made by manufacturer-sponsored fixtures and graphics; becoming "shops within the shop" of major retailers. According to the designers of this vendor shop, "the presence of Lee's Kids shop had to create a successful impact for the Lee's brand while carefully integrating within an existing department store design scheme." The wall presentation had to coordinate with the existing soffit and display approach and "decisions regarding custom fixtures had to consider the ability to enhance the Lee's brand as well as visually co-exist with J.C. Penney's store fixturing."

Medium and light wood tones were used consistently — "building on a design language of materials and shapes that had been introduced in other Lee's presen-tations." The overall design and materials of the fixtures needed to enhance the bright coloration of the product as well as convey their "down-to-earth" price positioning. All together, the shop had to make a statement about the value, quality, and affordability of the Lee product.

The fixtures were designed to present graphic information that explains features like fit, fabric, etc. Shelf Talkers introduce size, name and silhouette information so that shoppers don't have to unfold the garments to get the answers to their questions. In addition, the fixtures needed to meet Lee's requirement for "product on the floor to meet the product-turn goals" and also had to be able to change over when products were updated or shifted. This vendor shop design was a recent winner in the national ISP contest in the shop within a department store category.

STRIDE RITE

Randall Park Mall, N. Randall, OH

The Stride Rite Shoe Co. is a nationally recognized manufacturer and retailer of children's shoes with outlets in over 250 malls across the country. In an effort to keep the customers they have and gain more potential customers in malls overwhelmed with sports shoes shops, the company commissioned G. Herschman Architects of Cleveland, OH to come up with a bright, new, and colorful prototype for future Stride Rite stores.

This 1,200 sq. ft. space is typical of mall spaces nsually occupid by Stride Rite stores. Here, the designers have showcased the small scale merchandise with a strong, coordinated background of neutral colored slatwall, vividly colored accents and complementary graphics. Adding to the fun and vitality of the space is a fun house mirror, video and even a play wall for the kids.

"The ceiling breaks the focus of the eye to the merchandise by setting a playful 'squiggle' along one edge of the store." The carpet on the floor is made up of the bright accent colors used on the walls but the small overall pattern seems to "anchor" the carpet which provides a "solid platform" for the store's layout. To open up the space even more, the open back show windows manage to extend the store to the mall line while still presenting a distinct window display and entrance effect.

"The store expresses a colorful, kid-oriented shopping atmosphere that can make an often trying experience into an enjoyable one."

KIDSFUN

Northdale Court, Tampa, FL

Design: Pavlik Design Team, Ft. Lauderdale, FL
Photographer: Myroslav Rosky

According to the designers of this 12,000 sq. ft. play-center, "Kidsfun is an exciting futuristic playground that's here today." The basic concept behind Kidsfun is a play area that will encourage children to develop skills — use their imagination and exercise their minds and bodies through hands-on experiences. It is also a place where children can have parties in private rooms or participate in just fun activities.

To attract people from the main boulevard, a three story kite-shaped entry was created that is illuminated for full impact. "A colorful store front with undulating walls and bold entrances entices visitors to this very special experience." Within, bold shapes and bright colors and patterns abound. The unusually shaped space features zig-zag walls, snaking shapes and skewered aisles that invite the kids to explore an array of fun zones.

A colorful clock tower, checkered floor and zig-zag fence leads the kids to the Kidsfun Cafe and Treats concession area where the counters and displays of the "cool stuff" merchandise and prizes are uniquely designed at children's heights. For kids who have special parties here, there are Party Houses with angled walls, bubble windows and funky birthday thrones. For the other kids this is a world of games, rides, and fun within "a dazzling environment created just for them."

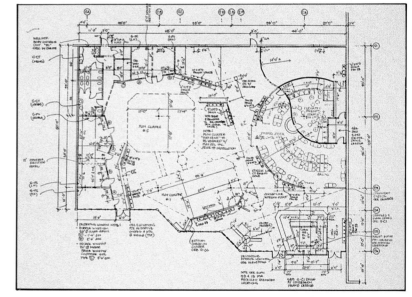

"Extensive research and planning to detail went into making this play center unique and better than anything before. Relaxation in a plush, glass enclosed parent's lounge which is centrally located, offers worry-free, maximum visibility as well as peace and quiet." This is definitely the "playground of tomorrow" for today's mall-oriented children.

ARTS & KIDS

Mall of America, Bloomington, MN

Design: Shea Architects, Minneapolis, MN

Located on the main level in the North Garden of the giant Mall of America is this delightfully inviting, child-oriented store of 1,078 sq. ft. The owners of Arts & Kids are committed to the education of children through art and with that purpose foremost, they have stocked the open space with kits, games, books and art supplies. The architects/designers, Shea Architects, have taken the space and the stock and turned it into a hands-on adventure for the thousands of kids who move through the mall almost daily.

The sign that floats over the bright, white space is full of color and features an artist's palette and a G-clef that serves as an ambersand. An undulating wave moves around the three interior walls of the space with hidden lights illuminating the ceiling above. The white laminate slatwall floor fixtures and the white shelving on the walls are lit by the incandescent spots on tracks that gird the space and also by those embedded in the ceiling.

Adding to the sweep of the store and also creating a playful path is the white floor striped with red, yellow, and blue — the same primary colors that appear in the signage in the front. The rear part of the store is carpeted in deep blue.

"Large geometric forms introduce the building foun-
dation of education" and dominos, videos and artwork
at the store's front are meant to entice the passersby.
What the kids seem to enjoy the most is the freedom of
graffiting the washable white surface of the cash/wrap
desk — and the drawing materials are made available
to them.

P.B. PAGES BOOK STORE

Mall of America, Bloomington, MN

Design: Kiku Obata & Coi., St. Louis, MO
Photographer: MMP/RVC

B. Dalton Bookseller, a division of Barnes & Noble, Inc. unveiled its prototype bookstore for children in the Mall of America. It is the 3,500 sq. ft. P.B. Pages store illustrated here. "We wanted to create a bookstore for children where books come alive in a store bursting with images and ideas," said Maureen Golden, V.P. General Merchandise Manager for B. Dalton Booksellers.

The noted graphic designer, Kiku Obata who also created the outstanding graphics program for the Mall of America, was entrusted with creating the space and the image. The store does appeal to children of all ages as well as their parents and grandparents.

From without, the children are drawn to the space by the imaginative doorway which is "constructed" of seven 11' and 13' "books" stacked to create a post and lintel entrance into the store. The two books that flank the entrance have recognizable characters from children's books (Harold and Lyle, the Crocodile) emerging from between the pages.

Upon entering the store, the children and their parents are led through the warm, wood-toned space along a winding path of maple flooring strewn with handscreened letters that leads past various "landmarks" located in the store and around the bookcases.

The most notable and noticeable of the landmarks is the focal point, a 15' book tower with Dr. Seuss characters peeking out from the purple glass windows on top.

Soaring overhead like giant butterflies are "flying books" suspended from the ceiling. As passengers in this flight to fancies there are favorite book characters like Madeline and Curious George. Along the far end of the space is a library for 8-12 year olds which features trees covered with leaves and book pages. Everywhere book pillows have been provided and the children are invited to sit down and read the books displayed. On the walls there are quotes like, "Everytime a child reads a book — the world opens up."

All the fixtures, bookcases, gondolas and landmarks are constructed of select northern maple with a clear finish or a tinted stain. A warm color palette of the maple and white, yellow, orange, green and purple — in muted tones — was chosen to appeal to both the parents and the children. According to Kiku Obata, "We tried to create a timeless and classic character for P.B. Pages. The result is a warm, sophisticated and whimsical bookstore that invites children of all ages and their parents to enter into the imaginative world of books."

ANIMALIA

Mall of America, Bloomington, MN

Design: Shea Architects, Minneapolis, MN

In a mall of wonders, one very special wonder to children and adults alike is Animalia, and especially the sculptured facade that stops the shoppers in this mall of many attractions and "stoppers." In contrast to all the slick and polished facades around it, the rough hewn, stoney and craggy surface of Animalia is unique. To either side of the wide opening into the almost totally white store are a pair of "gargoyle" heads with gaping "mouths" that become the display cases for the store. A local sculptor, Chris Tulley, created this "Easter Island lost village" look for the exterior of Animalia. The product lines exhibited within all have one thing is common — the commonality is Animals.

Displayed inside the store on assorted white laminate cubes, in and on the semi-circular glazed counter/sales desk and on the broken, battered hulk of a wrecked ship that dominates the floor are sculpted, painted and assemblages of animals — wild and tame. The aforementioned ship also serves as the major displayer/merchandiser in the shop with the white walls and blacked-out ceiling. Strung across that open ceiling are rows and rows of electrical tracks filled with incandescent spots that brilliantly show off the fabulous colors on the pieces displayed on the risers and on the walls.

Though the space is only 900 sq. ft. it seems larger due to the white ambience, the lighting and the carefully organized presentation of products.

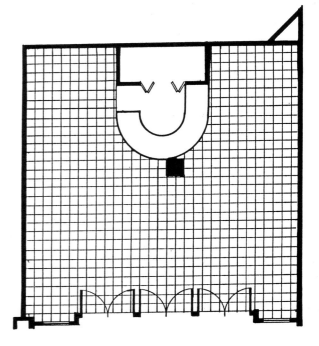

CELEBRATE BALTIMORE

Harborplace, Baltimore, MN

Design: The Office of Alexia N.C. Levite, Washington, DC

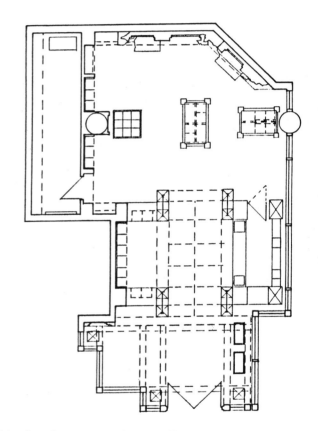

One of the top tourist attractions in Baltimore is the Harborside cluster near the waterfront and no visitor or "tourist" can be there without wanting to bring home some part of that experience. Celebrate Baltimore is a theme souvenir shop and the main challenges presented to the design firm of the 800 sq. ft. were:

1. Create a store front presence which would draw customers to the dead-end location in the mall.
2. Integrate the various "images of Baltimore" presented's products into a cohesive store theme.
3. Create an ordered store design in the irregular space.
4. Make maximum use of the limited space.

Using a custom designed store front and an exterior that recalls the facades of Baltimore's historic row houses with their marble steps, the designers were able to develop a store theme around the city of Baltimore. Assorted panels on the walls show off the city's rich cultural heritage, its neighborhoods, and industries.

A typical Baltimore row house was scaled down to fit into the store's display area. In order to position the facade within the store, the designers used a "crumbling away" effect; the modern day store's walls "crumble away" to reveal what might have been seen on this spot in years past. A painted screen door — the pride of

Polish neighborhoods — is authentically reproduced for the setting. A soft sculpture of a gossiping woman in a second story window adds "neighborhood flavor and humor while providing a means to display some of the store's merchandise."

Architecturally, an overhead trellis helps to define the central entryway and the circulation path. It is flanked on the right by a sales counter and on the left by a clothing display. Niches help to offset the displays — bringing order to a store that carries a lot of different kinds of merchandise.

On the interior, all of the ductwork was left exposed and the designers took as much height as they could to make the small store appear larger. Throughout they used polomyx paint, brick, plastic laminates, tinted glass on the store front, and drywall construction techniques.

CAESAR'S WORLD RETAIL STORE

The Forum Shops at Caesar's Palace, Las Vegas, NV

Design: TSL / Merchant Design Group, Los Angeles, CA
President: Tak Toda
Principal-in-Charge / Designer: Richard Lewis
Interior Design: Darra Brakefield
Architect: Andreas Cardennes, AIA, Los Angeles, CA
Special Effects: Pantone

The flying dice and the stacks of coins are only two of the sporting icons that appear in the store's design. On the floor is the giant roulette wheel executed in assorted imported Italian marbles and the roulette wheel motif is also carried out on the ceiling.

"Our purpose with Caesar's World store design was to attract customers with an adult toy — a fantasy-filled reflection of the Casino decor — which we see as light-hearted."

The designers of the space in the noted Greco-Roman Forum Shops wanted to capture the spirit and essence of "gaming attractions, great sporting events and other entertainments so unique to Caesar's." This is the first major retail store to be located outside of the Casino and the designers — working within the classic Caesar's framework added "contemporary, crowd-pulling, energetic, and whimsical design in the form of overscaled gambling icons such as the roulette wheel in the entrance floor.

A sky painted ceiling set off with sequential lighting is reflected in the longitude and latitude lines of the roulette wheel on the floor. The wheel is executed in imported Italian marbles with sequentially flashing tivoli bulbs. The colored bands that re-inforce the raised dome also add to the roulette wheel imagery in the design.

A "tower of dice" fixture turns into an aerial flight for oversized playing cards, outlined in neon, that float up to the ceiling and overscaled stacks of chips serve as fixtures and pedestals for display forms.

A star performer in this mix of modern and antique mayhem is Nero; a sculptured Segal-like statue who performs in various parts of the store. Up front he can be seen fiddling while behind him "the disintegrating colosseum smolders." He is also seen emulating the headline making feat of a noted daredevil — flying a motorbike over the Caesar's fountain. Even in the boxing ring we can see Nero working out and above him a ring of TV monitors show clips from outstanding sports events that have taken place at Caesar's Palace.

Black and white is used predominantly on the floors — on the faux marble columns and on the fixtures that stand on the floor or set between the columns on the walls. Gold leaf enrichment is seen everywhere. This project was the grand prize winner in the recent NASFM retail design contest for spaces under 10,000 sq. ft.

The service counter and one of the neon outlined flying cards overhead.

The flying bike trick (above left) as performed by the white Nero. The merchandise is stacked on black lacquered floor fixtures and wall units set beneath the arches and between the columns.

White columns enriched with gold rise up to support the sky painted, domed ceiling. In the boxing ring is Nero and above him the TV monitors show clips of past outstanding sporting events that took place at Caesar's Palace.

SPACE TRADERS

Space Center, Houston, TX

Designer: Sunderland Interspace Design, Inc., Vancouver, BC Canada
Base Bldg Architects: Waisman Dewar Grout Carter, Inc., Vancouver, BC and Pierce Goodwin Alexander & Linville, Houston, TX
Photographer: Milroy McAlber, Costa Mesa, CA

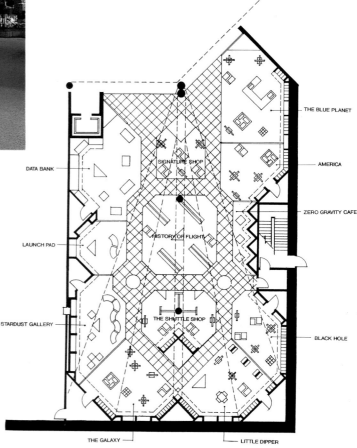

Space Traders is a 6,000 sq. ft. space in the 180,000 sq. ft. Space Center in Houston, TX where visitors to NASA's Mission Control come to experience and learn about the space industry.

The souvenir/gift shop offers sophisticated merchandise associated with the space industry and NASA didn't want the store to be like a Hollywood version of space travel. "Emphasis was placed on creating a realistic environment and not somebody's imaginative interpretation of what space or space travel should be." Working with the Marriott Corp., the designers planned the store as a series of boutique environments each themed appropriately for the merchandise presented. "The plan subtly controls the flow of the customers through the space, exposing them to a very organized presentation of attractive products."

A dynamic Delta wing ceiling — derived from the paper airplane — draws the shopper to the open entrance along with the display presentations up front. Once inside, the Data Bank on the right is where visitors can find the book department and just beyond is the stationery area which is called Launch Pad. Other departments or boutiques include Stardust Gallery (gifts), Little Dipper (kids), Black Hole (novelty), Zero Gravity (cafe-packaged foods), and Blue Planet (the environment).

Generally the color scheme is mostly black and gray. The gray is used on the free-standing fixtures, wall units and the Delta wing ceiling. The gray is metallic and thus suggests space craft and technology without competing or conflicting with the colors of the merchandise. Another significant color in the scheme is blue, which is part of the corporate identity of NASA and it is also used an accent color throughout the Base Building facility.

"The concept for Space Traders is to create a contemporary, dramatic, organized backdrop to a variety of interesting and unique souvenirs and gifts in a visually appealing environment capable of handling high velocity traffic."

LOONEY TUNES, USA

Six Flags Over Texas, Arlington, TX

Design: Space Design International, Los Angeles, CA
Account Executive: Jerry Gelsomino
Design Director: Linda Kreuger
Designer: Julie White
Project Manager: George Romero
Art Director: Kiran Raj Bhandary
Graphic Designer: Steve Gross
Lighting Designer: David Apfel

To house the wild and wacky cartoon characters who have appeared in the Looney Tunes cartoons, this 6,000 sq. ft. space was designed by Space Design International of Los Angeles, CA. It "combines bold colors, wacky perspective, trompe l'oeil murals and two or three dimensional characters to create a cartoon environment." Adding to the illusion that shoppers have stepped into a cartoon are the banks of video screens, showing Looney Tunes cartoons, that have been strategically placed throughout the store.

This store is located in Six Flags Over Texas — a giant theme entertainment/amusement center in Arlington, TX. Since everyone who visits Six Flags is potentially a Looney Tunes customer, the SDI design team made the store as energetic and engaging as the theme park's other attractions. To integrate the store with the park, the designers interspersed exciting videos of the rides and other attractions among the cartoons showing on the multiple screens.

The store is divided into three "rooms" each decorated as a different cartoon environment. The first area is decorated like a theater since most of the souvenirs and T-shirts found here bear the images of Bugs Bunny, Donald Duck and Elmer Fudd, who often appear on stage in their cartoons. In the next room where children's toys and apparel is on display, the space resembles a "typical home" where Tweetie Bird and Sylvester are usually found doing mischief. The desert motif of the last room comes right out of the Road Runner and Wile E. Coyote cartoons, and here is housed the higher end merchandise for adults, better quality gifts, and artwork.

The design of each room is fleshed out through an elaborate series of drawings and multi-dimensional figures "all erected with wacky humor, distorted perspective and playful logic of a Looney Tunes cartoon." Everything from the lighting to the signage to the fixtures to the choice of colors and materials was carefully chosen to contribute to the overall cartoon effect.

WARNER BROS. STUDIO STORE

Mall of America, Bloomington, MN

Design: Jon Greenberg Associates, Southfield, MI

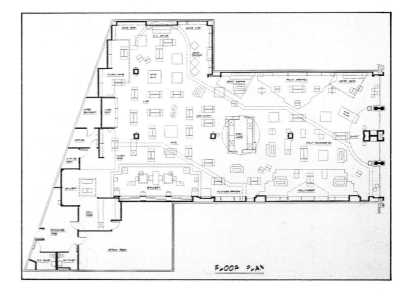

One of the most attracting and drawing stores appearing in the malls today is the Warner Bros. Studio Store and children of all ages can't wait to get through those gates. This is the gigantic Warner Bros. Studio Store that was revealed in the Mall of America — an entertainment/concept store that is guaranteed fun to shop.

"The store front has a central focus on the simulated grandeur of Hollywood Deco to complement the mall's theme." The grand entrance is contrasted with the dimensional, whimsical giant three dimensional characters Bugs Bunny, Daffy and Sylvester who greet the shoppers out in the mall's aisle. Once inside the store, the shopper is confronted with "amusement, amazement — and fun." Realistic character models gaze and beckon from atop floor fixtures, from the walls, dropping down from the ceiling or "busting through blockades." A blackened, exposed ceiling adds the "studio backlot" feeling to the space which is further highlighted by floating ceiling drops painted white. Nonfunctional but original kleig lights are suspended down among the HID theatrical lighting that is used for

authentic atmosphere. The up front marble flooring transitions into floors of natural wood planking accented with colored floor strips and geometric marble patterns. Brass stars are also embedded in the floor and out in the mall and they carry the names of famous Warner Bros. characters.

The space is divided into category boutiques which include Looney Tunes (adult wear), Tiny Toones (children's and infant's), D.C. Comics, Gallery Items, and Hollywood. Suspended from the ceiling in the middle of all this is the red circular Warner Bros. logo.

The entire fixturing package was custom designed in natural stained maple and black veneers. Most of the components are modular and can be made to accommodate various product categories. All the metal hardware is powder coated black with hang rods capped with the Warner Bros. shield. The Gallery area is more upscaled in its treatment. Burled wood trimmed with black lacquered accents, marble patterns and sliding wall panels effectively present the sequined apparel, memorabilia, and the framed celluloid stills.

A nine-screen video wall at the rear runs laser programmed reels of cartoons, Hollywood clips and out-takes while a Magical Tree allows children to "paint" computer pictures with the touch of the screen. There are even holographic performances of the cartoon characters. Without a doubt, this tore has met the "extraordinary challenge of retail merchandising and image presentation" successfully.

Home
Fashions
&
Accessories

ZONA

Tokyo, Japan

Design: Junji Yoshikawa
Engineering Fuji Co. Ltd. and Zona Design
Visual Merchandising: Louis E. Sagar / Mutsuko Ishikura
Photographer: Masayuki Sato, Cube Co. Ltd.

Zona first opened in Soho, in NYC in 1979 as a home furnishing and accessories store specializing in the Santa Fe look. All the products were a unique blend of Native American and Latin American cultures and even today they are made in Santa Fe. According to the Zona concept, it is based on the pristine simplicity of American Southwestern taste but with the added flavor of refined Italian Tuscan and more generally European country style. "Zona is constantly in pursuit of a 'natural vision' that allows style with the shackles of convention."

The first Zona in Japan opened in Tokyo in 1988 and we are presenting here the newly relocated and much larger Zona store designed by Engineering Fuji Co. working with the Zona design staff.

The more than 2,000 sq. ft. space is divided into "rooms" which are delineated by thick painted walls. The walls not only separate, they add to the charm and character of each setting. There is a series of vignette displays which represent a living room, dining room, kitchen, den, children's room, and garden — "each corner presents and develops a different life-setting." The overall ambience is warm and friendly and relaxed; the shopper is made to feel as though he or she was in the comfortable home of a friend.

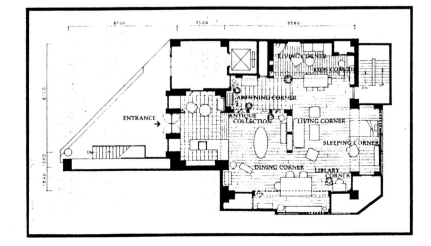

The design firm feels that by eliminating all standard or even custom fixturing and by using lifestyle visual merchandising techniques, they have allowed the merchandise "to structure the interior space." Displays are changed as soon as a piece in a group is sold so the customer is always given a new and fresh impression of the Zona look and line.

"You feel at ease the moment you enter as the interior's harmony of colors and peaceful atmosphere soothes the mind." Lighting was used with "the utmost attention around the windows and doors so that even the shadows cast by plants become suggestive parts of the design. This orchestrated use of line, color, and light gives the shop itself a natural sort of healing effect."

Indeed, this is internationalization of design: American Southeast aesthetics and classical Florentine overtones with the Japanese mystical sensitivity to color, line and light.

DOUGLASS & WATERS

King of Prussia Mall, King of Prussia, PA

Design: Jon Greenberg Associates, Southfield, MI

The concept was to create a home furnishings store that would "feel home-like" and also communicate the essence of "home." Through extensive research, the designers, Jon Greenberg Associates, opted for a store with an English Country style — blended with an American accent; "not rustic, but refined." The challenge also was to design a store with a high-style country attitude that would be flexible enough to adapt to future industry directions.

The client felt the need for a strong merchandise presentation on the leaseline, visible from a distance and the store front design with a recessed entrance flanked by bay windows with cranberry colored mullions not only did that but it also created a "residential feeling." In the first "room" is visible an array of fabric samples which "generate ideas and excitement" while the work tables communicate a designer's presence which is what the client wanted.

The eclectic collection of furniture is organized in an uncluttered environment so that views from the mall through the wide windows offer visual layers through a series of rooms — each with its own focal point. The store's plan also had to be flexible to accommodate a three tier delivery system; in-stock, quick-custom, and designer-custom. Large areas are also set aside for the display of window treatments, comforters and the extensive fabric selection with customer friendly tables.

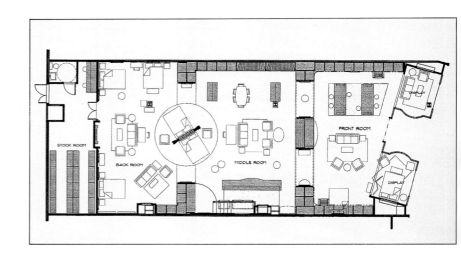

The interior of the store is cranberry and white with accents of brass along with birch wood stained medium brown which is used for the case goods and architectural elements. The floor is a combination of natural sisal-like carpeting which contrasts with the wood areas. To add to the residential feel, the lighting is primarily incandescent with softly dramatic high and low levels. A dimmer system adjusts for seasonal and merchandise variations.

THE CONRAN SHOP

Left Bank, Paris, France

Design: Euro RSCG Design Agora Sopha
Principal in Charge: Roland Leu
Project Design: Frederique Sebaoun / Steve Arnold
Photographer: Jean Philippe Caulliez

The building which contains the three levels of selling space in 13,500 sq. ft. is located on the smart and stylish Left Bank of Paris — just steps off the Blvd. St. Germain. Its look and design are in keeping with the tradition and spirit of the now famous London shop of the same name. The designers set out to create as spacious a shop as possible and they turned to their advantage "the constraints made by the structure which inspired the sculpting of different sales areas." One of the major elements required was the construction of a vast stairwell that would serve to link up the three retail levels of the store.

The Conservatory area, located below street level, does get some natural light from windows overlooking a narrow courtyard. This area is devoted to garden furniture and accessories. The outdoors theme is reflected in the design and in the terra cotta tiled floor which adds to the warm, earthy atmosphere.

Set out on an oak parquet floor — on the first level up — is the furniture and soft furnishings. Special attention was given to the lighting so that different ambiences could be affected for the different room settings being shown.

The all-important ground level of the store flows freely and fluidly around a circular central atrium. Here the shoppers will find accessories and gifts for the many different lifestyles of various family members.

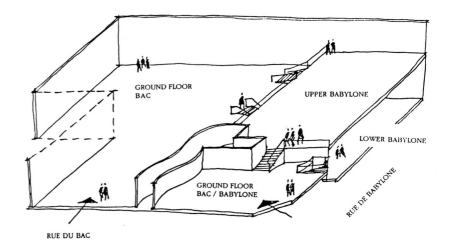

The gypsum plaster ceiling is studded with bright spots which also help to visually organize the space.

All the display and presentation systems were custom built of the finest materials. The sweep of the curvaceous sycamore veneered wall is repeated in the arc of the cash/wrap desk and some of the presentation niches. "The overall impression is one of cool, uncluttered calm."

An interesting note: The facade of the building was restored to the original design of Gustave Eiffel of Eiffel Tower fame.

DE BIJENKORF

Amsterdam, The Netherlands

One of the floor-to-ceiling merchandising walls with a small storage below each vertical unit. Wood and metal ladders glide along the track set above 2 ft. down from the ceiling which gives the salesperson access to the products on the upper shelves.

Design: Virgile & Stone, London, England

de Bijenkorf is the leading Dutch department store with six branches in Holland and it is also one of Europe's most successful department store operations.

In the Amsterdam flagship store, Virgile & Stone, which has a long association with de Bijenkorf, have developed a new design scheme for the 3,000 sq. metres household, textiles and furniture floor which includes 18 different product groupings. "The concept of integrating diverse areas of merchandise whilst still maintaining individual departments represents a new approach to the way the merchandise stories are presented and displayed," says the design team.

The Home Textile area has just recently been completed and opened, and it represents the first stage of this project. The designers have integrated innovative visual merchandising with strong colors within a modern, yet relaxed, environment. "By allowing daylight into the department, we have achieved a natural 'home' ambience which encourages customers to make their color decisions with confidence."

The space is neutral in color — filled with the daylight and with flattering incandescent light which falls upon the light, natural colored woods. Some of the floor fixtures are fabricated of that wood and there are wall areas which are completely shelved or lined with the same pleasant colored wood.

Another towel display. The wood wall with predrilled holes serves as a giant peg board and the pegs can be used to show off towels, wash clothes and even the wire grid can be attached to the wall panel. Note how the towels are displayed — folded, draped, and rolled.

DOMAIN

Freehold Raceway Mall, Freehold, NJ

Design: Bergmeyer Associates, Inc., Boston, MA
Partner in Charge: Joseph P. Nevin, Jr.
Planners: Michael R. Davis, AIA / Jeanne Carey, AIA /
  Robert Nardone
Project Manager / Job Captain: Jeanne Carey, AIA
For Domain: Bill Reardon, Visual Merchandising
Photographer: Chun Y. Lai, New York, NY

Domain burst upon the home furnishings and fashion scene in the 1980s as a "progressive, discriminating furniture retailer" with a distinctly avant garde approach to store design. This new prototype design, by Bergmeyer Associates, presents a "warmer, more domestic context" for Domain's furniture and furnishings. The new look makes use of a coherent presentation set-up that starts at the store's entry and carries through to the bays along the wall and includes the choice of materials and finishes that are "compatible with the products' direction." For this design, the architects/designers refer to the earliest works in America of the great European modern architects like Van Der Rohe and Walter Gropius. They call it "Classic High Modern"; timeless, abstract and understated.

Light natural-finish maple with crisp, parallel grain in matched panels rotated 15 degrees was chosen as the featured wall finish. For an "easily repairable background surface" for hanging mirrors and decorative accessories, the designers selected a mottled, artistic paint finish of golds and taupes while the neutral

surfaces and piers were painted a warm white. Stainless steel picture rails and moveable panel hardware are used as are patined brass sheets to recall the client's taste for antiques and ironwork.

The store front and the first bay of the store's interior establish the feeling of a sophisticated domestic setting with rich natural wood, antiqued metal accents, warm colors and incandescent lighting targeted low in the room settings. Subsequent "room settings" are spacially separated by deep, simple box beams on the ceiling each equipped with stainless steel tracks for hanging relocatable wood veneered panels.

The prototype store front "was conceived as solids, voids, and planes, spacially challenging the lease line, with patined brass clad doors that pivot open to form planes perpendicular to the flow of traffic."

What the designers have achieved is a setting that allows each furniture vignette to "describe a distinct domestic setting within a harmonious, sophisticated and flexible setting."

FELISSIMO

E. 56th St., New York, NY

Design: Clodagh, NY
Architect: Robert Pierpont

Felissimo — a 30-year-old Japanese mail order company of housewares and clothing — took the opportunity to create a unique retail and architectural statement for their first store in New York when they commissioned Clodagh, the minimalist designer, to "recycle" a turn of the century, neoclassic townhouse into their flagship operation. "The utmost priority was to incorporate the historic baroque and rococo architectural details while restoring the building back to its original use as a gracious and tranquil home environment." Clodagh proceeded to create "a healthy space" using environmentally sound products and procedures in "an earthy elemental design style" for decor and furnishings.

The neoclassic facade of limestone has been stained a warm ochre color and a "concrete carpet" extends to the curb. Woven copper banners and fibre optic torches flank the entrance. The interior has been designed as a retreat from the pressures of the city. There is a garden room with fountains, a living room, a dining room, a bedroom, a dressing room, a tea-room, a library and an artspace. Each of these residential spaces is "fixtured" and furnished with items designed to complement the decor — enhance the merchandise displayed and also serve as saleable items. The home furnishings correspond to the room settings they would naturally appear in like the garden items in the garden room or the conservatory.

Clodagh selected a palette mainly composed of ochre, terra cotta and the sand colors. Sun bleached and sand

blasted wood tops were combined with patina-ed steel bases in autumn leaf colors. Also used are copper, cherrywood, cast bronze, khaki/clay colored concrete floors and fresco plaster on walls.

To integrate the existing architectural details, the sweeping spiral rococo staircase was completely restored as the centerpiece of the design. Most of the fashions are housed on the second floor white above the second the individual rooms were redesigned using a scheme of sculptural walls with dramatic painting and undulating display wall in terra cotta plaster for the third floor where the living and dining room items were presented. Daniel Bergluna, a lighting fixture designer, created the street sconces as well as two chandeliers and several small lights on the second floor. They are made of recycled industrial machine parts, car pieces and jet engines. "This recycling perfectly reflects Felissimo's environmental policy of reuse." The special tables, chairs and breakfront in the "dining room" were created by Geoffrey Warner and Alan Swansen and Elvin Hess of Architectural Sculpture Assoc. integrated wood, metal, concrete and bronze to fulfill Clodagh's design of a walk-up bookcase and papyrus.

"In keeping with Felissimo's philosophy, every aspect of the design and development of the store reflects a respect for environmental concerns. Non-toxic paints and finishes were used throughout, while recycled materials were used wherever possible."

TAKASHIMAYA

Fifth Ave., New York, NY

Architect: John Burgee Architects, New York, NY
Interior Design: Larry Laslo
Visual Merchandising Director: James Griffin
Photographer: MMP/RVC

The Takashimaya N.Y. limestone facade is appointed at street level by two, 32-foot columns of black granite which stand on seven foot tall pedestals of pink granite. The three story atrium can be seen through the open yet gridded window area and framing the gently bowed windows are black granite columns which start on the fourth floor.

For the store's interior, Larry Lazlo has redefined the meaning of "East meets West." He used inlaid marble floors, stucco Venetia, faux parchment, bronze, slate, padded linen for some walls, suede linings for display cases and gold and silver leafing to "create a timeless and international shopping environment."

Located on the main level — off the entrance — is the Terrace Boutique which is filled with flowers and garden-related items. The windows allow light to flood into this space which can be viewed from open balconies above the street level. One of the major art galleries is located behind the Terrace Boutique and the entire second floor is also devoted to the showing of art.

The third, fourth and fifth levels — a total of 20,500 sq. ft. of space — is reserved for retailing. The third level is devoted to Takashimaya Home Design. In the residentially-scaled store interior, the cross cultural theme of Takashimaya is developed and displayed. Employing design details and elements from Italy, London, New York, Tokyo, and Hong Kong — coordinated with antique and modern furnishings — the designers have "created an eclectic, neo-classic ambience." Vignetted settings of various areas in the home are set up in the handsome open landscape of the third floor to show off the coordinated merchandise.

The store stocks a diverse array of merchandise many of which are designed exclusively for Takashimaya. The products range from home furnishings and home fashion accessories to table and bed linens, specialty gifts, objets d'art — and, of course, the paintings and sculptures that appear in the 4500 sq. ft. galleries on the first and main levels. The all-important gallery is accessed by the attractive multi-level atrium which is "the architectural centerpiece of the building. The inclusion of the gallery — which reflects an expressly Japanese retailing structure — coupled with the dedication to customer service will distinguish Takashimaya N.Y. as one of the most exceptional retail ventures."

Hiroshi Hidaka, the president of the 163 year old company which began in Kyoto in 1831 as a kimono shop, had this to say about this new store.

"The N.Y. store aims to be a new type of buisiness — something different from stores Takashimaya has operated thus far. The unifying concept is a cross-cultural weaving of East and West. Takashimaya will select exquisite design elements from around the world and incorporate them into a unique selection of products available only in Takashimaya N.Y."

SHERIDAN STYLE, HARROD'S

London, England

Design: Four IV, London, England

The fabric cutting station (left) and the cash desk are set off by the specially woven blue carpet bordered with a fine gold swirl pattern. The ceiling overhead is coffered.

Sheridan, the international home fashions company, has further strengthened its market position with the introduction of a unique, flagship department within Harrod's — London's world-famous department store. Within the allotted 2200 sq. ft. of Harrod's linen department, the designers, Four IV, while acknowledging the established retail identity, were still able to create a "look" to cater to the ranges available within the store.

An oak floor defines the specific space and bleached beech was used extensively for the merchandising system. Etched glass and fine bronze and nickel detailing along with soft neutral colors complete the color and materials palette. A sophisticated network of directional downlighters — recessed into the ceiling — enable the merchandise to be highlighted on the floor fixtures and the four specially designed, hand blown glass and nickel chandeliers provide the ambient light — and separates the Sheridan area from the rest of the linen department. Etched glass panels within the perimeter cabinets subtly illuminate the products on the shelves and on the ceiling a recessed band of illuminated etched glass plus small brass downlights allows maximum lighting effects on the merchandise displayed within the perimeter.

A specially commissioned rug — woven in Sheridan blue with a fine gold swirl border design — is used to accentuate the location of the cash/wrap and fabric cutting station and another rug marks out the fabric consultation table. Special attention was paid to the dramatic bed displays which appear on the oak floor of the shop.

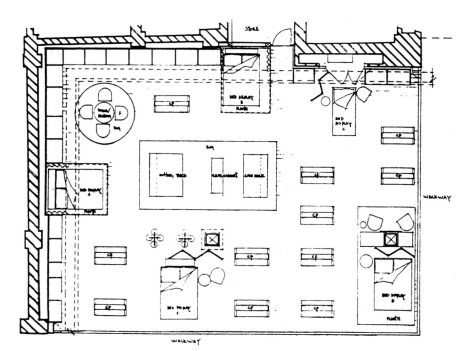

A view of Sheridan's boutique (above) on the linen floor of Harrod's. The four specially designed chandeliers mark off the space which is further delineated by the oak floor.

Another special rug in Sheridan blue is laid beneath the fabric consultation table where customers can interact with trained personnel. This "homey" vignette is similar to the bed displays which are embellished with "carpeted plinths, trompe l'oeil back drops and flamboyant canopies."

FABERGE

Bloomingdales, Lexington Ave., New York, NY

Design: Fitzpatrick Design Group, New York, NY
Jay Fitzpatrick, President and Creative Director
Gerald Brienza, V.P. of Project
Enrique Montalvo, Designer
Lisa Benson, Director of Colors & Materials

Located on the auspicious sixth floor of the Bloomingdales flagship store is this tiny boutique. "The Great Faberge" and "The Art of the Jeweler to the Imperial Court of Russia" are two expressions that stimulated the design of this small, yet classically detailed, China shop. It sits in a gray/white envelop which is common to all the "boutiques" clustered on this floor.

To showcase the Faberge collection, Fitzpatrick Design Group has created some exquisite architectural armoires in which to present the products. The armoires, designed to depict "The Great Age of Faberge," stand side by side to create the shop. The pieces are constructed of wood and finished with black lacquer. The crown moldings and the column pilasters are gold leafed and the columns also act as dividers between the openings. The furniture "depicts the design flair of the classical perimeter" and the Lucifer lights, hidden behind the column of the armoire, illuminate the collectible pieces.

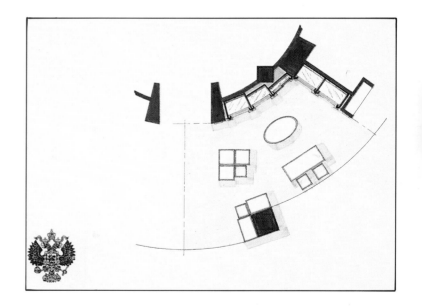

PUEBLO SPIRIT

Mall of America, Bloomington, MN

Design: Shea Architects, Minneapolis, MN

This small, 787 sq. ft. space — off in a corner of the vast Mall of America, still manages to attract shoppers to the unique store that sells home fashion accessories as well as costume accessories all filled with the Pueblo of Native American spirit.

The space is rich in texture and atmosphere which together creates a special kind of shopping experience. The floor is laid with odd shaped stones in a haphazard pattern and the thick, rough surfaced, sand stuccoed walls are sculptural in feeling. Sawn off timbers and the stony niches that look like adobe walls create the display areas along the perimeter walls of the shop. Native drums become decorative risers on the floor and the single displayer/counter out in the center of the floor is also drum-like in design.

Hanging down from the high, blacked-out ceiling are cloud-like panels painted with symbols, signs and pictograms of Indian heritage. The artwork is done in turquoise, terra cotta, black and white. These floating shapes add a sense of intimacy to the space while they also add to the "spirit" of the store. Set in the blacked-out ceiling are the electric tracks that carry the focusable spots used to highlight the merchandise on the glass shelves inside the architectural perimeter units as well as the material resting above the cases.

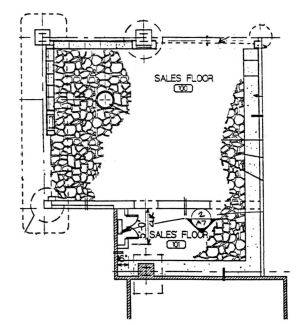

Potpourri

MONTEREY BAY AQUARIUM GIFT & BOOK SHOP

Monterey Bay Aquarium, Monterey, CA

Design: J.T. Nakaoka Associates, Architects, Los Angeles, CA
Principal in Charge: James "Jas" Nakaoka
Project Manager: Maxie Karimian
Team: Elizabeth Howley / Patricia Flower
V.M. Team: Bill Townsend / Gail Gonzales / Michelle Fry / Mark Gibson / Michelle McKenzie / Janet Wilkins

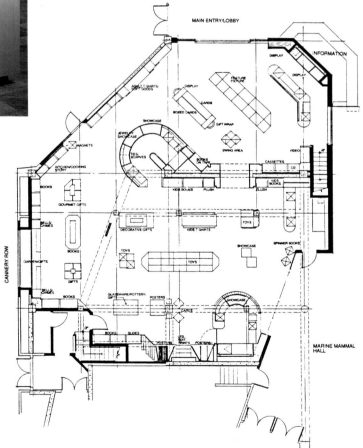

This, the main gift and book store of the Monterey Bay Aquarium — set in the historic and picturesque Cannery Row written about by John Steinbeck — is an irregularly shaped space of about 3,275 sq. ft. The client wanted the design and plan to be "timeless in image" as well as emphasize and enhance the educational experience of those visiting the aquarium. The "mood" was to be "clean, open, informal and comfortable" — yet warm and friendly to contrast with the gray and cold look of the aquarium itself.

Since the store had to be able to accommodate 2,500 to 3,000 shoppers during the peak hours of the season, a wide main aisle was created that lures the shopper to the rear of the store past a selection of impulse items. At the end is the large and bright Cannery Row window. To quickly dissipate and spread out the shoppers at peak times, secondary internal focal points were created. A few art images and books are visually prominent directly at eye level, in the path of the shopper's initial core of vision. "This also partially helps to accommodate to the ease of seasonal/thematic display changes with a few changes of art images." The fixture configuration and placement make maximum use of the irregularly shaped space and also helps to open up secondary aisle spaces. The circulation patterns encourage a complete traffic flow through the store.

Figured, white maple veneer was selected as the primary finish and the maple wood bathed in the bright incandescent light provides a neutral and complementary frame for the merchandise. Muted green colored, powder coated, steel accents with a touch of stainless steel impart "complementary but subtle sophistication to the raw industrial look of the environment."

Colored, perforated metal ceilings were used for acoustical control, however, the light color also makes the very low ceiling of the space seem visually more inviting as the shoppers enter from the adjacent space with its 30 ft. ceiling. "Its linear emphasis virtually organizes the ever changing placement of lighting fixtures and also helps to direct the shoppers towards the rear of the store."

MUSEUM STORE

Natural History Museum of Los Angeles, Burbank, CA

Design: James T. Nakaoka Associates, Architects, Los Angeles, CA

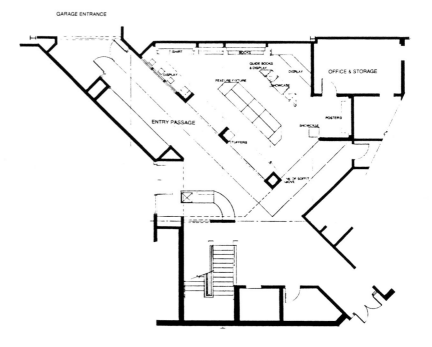

We have seen a trend towards "museum shops" — not only in the malls across the country but also in the art and natural history museums, in aquariums (as shown in the previous entry), and in other areas which are receiving less and less financial support from the local and federal governments. It helps them to sustain the museum or opera company or whatever, while it also is "the last and only opportunity for a museum to prolong the learning experience of the visitors and make it possible for the visitors to take a part of the museum experience home." Since we have become a nation of "souvenir hunters," the museum shops offer us more upscaled and upgraded and more "educational" mementos.

For this museum store in the Natural History Museum of Los Angeles, the objective was to create a store within a limited budget that would be warm and relaxed in ambience, quiet and dignified in appearance yet appealing to the particular target market. Since the store was scaled down to the 10 to 15 year-old shoppers (mainly), it also had to be able to withstand the wear and tear inflicted by this age group on the furnishings. The "Discovery Center" would be changing its exhibits frequently and this 655 sq. ft. space would have to be flexible and adjust to the changes in mix and quantity of product.

The center and heart of the store is the multi-leveled feature display fixture which can accommodate a large volume of merchandise. It visually anchors the store. The perimeters of the store are designed with terraced display areas to accommodate merchandise ranging from books, T-shirts and educational materials, to mugs, card, sculptures, etc. Each fixture has its own interior storage space for stock.

The cabinets are constructed of wood for a warm, natural finish. The wood is gray-washed with a water borne polyurethane finish which produces a durable, maintenance free finish that also eliminates the careful color matching of the veneer woods. The main cash register desk has been designed so that the actual register is shielded from view but area is provided for brochure display and merchandise presentation.

BLEISTIFT & CO.

Neumunster

Design: Umdasch Shop-Concepts, Neidenstein, Germany

The designers took the 456 sq. meter (approx. 4,800 sq. ft.) space which was formerly a storage depot in an old industrial building and converted it into a retail facility for office supplies, office furniture, stationery and such. They also arranged for office space and stock rooms. The designers tried to preserve the basic "industrial" look of the structure while adding some charm and human amenities.

Originally, the store was meant to appeal to the wholesale buyers of office supplies, but the firm soon found itself attracting the retail buyers as well and thus more space was needed for the presentation of the many different categories of merchandise. Since there was no opportunity for getting any additional space, the designers had to improvise with the available space and with the Umdasch shopfitting techniques available to them.

The wall areas are mostly covered with the design firm's stepped shelf system and as floor fixtures they used H and X gondolas as well as the Umdasch Quatro-Line showcases units. The decorative system on the wall is white laminate outlined in bright red and red lacquered metal is used throughout on the floor systems. All of the signage — a most important element in this multi-product type of operation — is done in red or white or red on clear plastic.

The ceiling is criss-crossed with a pattern of fluorescent fixtures fitted with egg-crate baffles — all in white — with white housed spotlights attached to these fixtures to highlight the signage and the wall displays. A sturdy, industrial type broadloom carpet in charcoal, gray and red is used to add some graciousness to the hi-tech space. To make the space more inviting, there is a coffee corner set aside for the shoppers, and fresh flowers and plants enliven the space.

BUCHER ZENTRUM

Shopping City Sud, Vienna, Austria

Design: Umdasch Shop-Concepts, Amstetten, Germany
Sepp Schneider

For this 500 sq. meter (approx. 5,300 sq. ft.) space in Austria's largest shopping center, the designers developed "a specialized market concept with distinct priorities; clear overview, self information by the customer, and stimulating frontal presentation."

The floor is laid with creamy ceramic tiles and the light colored walls are almost completely hidden by the books arranged on the natural wood shelves. The framing of the shelf units is also wood as are the sometimes imaginative floor fixtures like the "train" shown in this view that transports reading pleasures for the young. The other floor gondolas are also of the warm, wood material combined with bright red metal trim and the occasional multi-tiered museum cases on

the floor (see far left rear) are also constructed of those two materials.

To add to the warm and inviting ambience and to encourage the shoppers to stay awhile, there is a profusion of real trees and plants that seem to be growing everywhere in this rather vast space.

According to the designers, "Books require low-level presentation and room has to be provided for customers with shopping trolleys (carts). The articles must be displayed forcefully." To accomplish these goals, the designers felt that the Umdasch bookshelf system with its diverse accessories was ideal since it makes possible simple and swift changes in presentation, stock arrangements and displays.

B&L PAPETERIE

Liege, Belgium

Taking up 400 sq. meters (approx. 4,225 sq. ft.) on two levels, B&L Papeterie is the largest book and stationery store in Liege. The large store is located in the city center and the lower level — the ground level — is dominated by a dramatic, floating metal staircase and thus the area is monochromatic and ranges from white to pale aqua-blue to bright and navy blue to black. The neutral floor is laid with light gray ceramic tiles.

The walls are equipped with slotted standards set between white laminate panels and the various shelves and cubicles are supported by metal brackets off the wall strips. The fixtures on the selling floor are based on the Umdasch "Libro" and "Vitrina" systems. The signing repeats the blue, aqua and white scheme and even on the unique showcase/cash desk in the rear the vitrine is aqua in the all-white laminate finished unit.

A white metal tube fitted with fluorescent lamps is suspended down around the cash desk and also around the landing of the blue metal staircase for extra ambient light while the ceiling is patterned with recessed fluorescent fixtures. A black track system carries mini-spots in black housings that light up the merchandise presented on the wall. The same fixtures are suspended down on rigid black metal rods and used to accentuate the products displayed on the rear wall behind the cash/wrap desk.

*Design: Umdasch Shop-Concepts, Neidenstein, Germany
Marc Bonamie of the Belgian Planning & Marketing
Bureau*

LEVEL ONE

Oxford Street, London, England

Design: Red Jacket, London, England

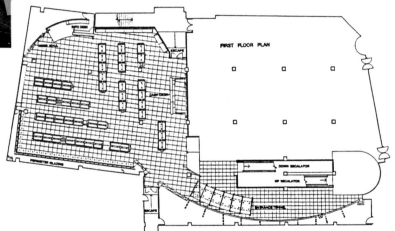

HMV, U.K., Ltd. requested that the design firm, Red Jacket, develop a computer games retail store that would not only set the standard for computer game retailing, but would also be unique in its field.

Level One is located one flight up in an existing HMV store on Oxford St. and in order to draw the shoppers to this area the designers developed a 35' curved wall which extends from the games store to the head of the escalators where the shoppers arrive. "The insertion of this element into a somewhat 'tired' environment has been accentuated by a grid of fibre optic tails that light through its vertical face."

The ceremonial entrance into Level One is a tunnel of tensile fabric stretched between elliptical steel ribs covering a stainless steel, perforated ramp which follows the curved wall into the department. "The translucent membrane has light, color, and imagery case on it from the outside to be viewed by the customers on their journey along the walkway." The actual arrival point coincides with the beginning of a central ceiling raft that carries downlights and air conditioning units and also acts as the main route for all high level power distribution. It also emphasizes the main thoroughfare of the shop and the mid floor merchandise units splay out from this walkway.

In order to capture the excitement of the games and the unpredictability of the games market, the designers developed a space "that has a built-in capacity to react to the order of the day"; a non-static environment.

It is done with lights! Housed behind a 25' long by 3' high translucent glass wall are 24 circuits of light combining 750 watts scanning projectors with more traditional colored fluorescents and low voltage spot lights. These are channeled back, via a dimming rack, to a "scene" setting computer which has been programmed to perform eight different scenes designed to be pro- as well as re-active. Ten colors can be individually selected to act as a backdrop to the projected images and branded messages that travel across the rear face of the glass. A line of fibre optic heads are set into the floor immediately in front of this wall to discourage customers from approaching the laminated glass panels.

Low level lamps highlight the products on the lower shelves while downlights illuminate the polished black vinyl floor. This is as high-tech an ambience as one could hope to see and right on target for the highly technical world of computer games.

KODAK'S RAHOLA IMAGE CENTER

Ponce, Puerto Rico

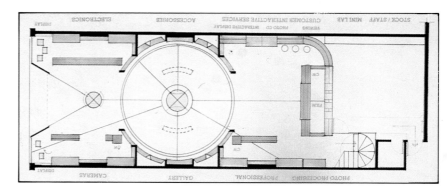

Design: Cato Gobe and Associates, Inc., New York, NY
President / CEO: Marc Gobe
Creative Director: Kenneth Hirst
Project Manager: Kyla Lange

Though most people think of Kodak as the leading brand of photographic film and supplies, the company has been purchasing film processing labs and retail outlets in Latin America. They recently acquired a local chain of processing stores called Rahola, in Puerto Rico, which led to the design of this new retail prototype design for the company in Ponce.

Cato Gobe, world famous graphic design firm was commissioned by Kodak and they set out to explore the concept of "imaging" in its evolving forms as a design platform for the new Kodak retail venture.

In this 1,800 sq. ft. space, a circular store layout was affected with a series of "boutiques" which create a "sense of discovery" throughout the store. Additional visual cues help the shoppers wind their way through the store to access the merchandise displays, rather than walk straight to the rear counter for film, then make a quick exit.

In the center of the focal point, inlaid into the floor are names of the various departments. Words were chosen to highlight particular products and to activate each category — like the word "capture" for Cameras and "appreciate" for albums. The individual departments are visually reinforced with back-lit murals whose "humorous images provide a fun and colorful counterpoint to each department." Colorful wall patterns are colored in a soft palette of greens, blues, and yellows.

Behind the portrait studio is a high-tech, all-white, light-filled film lab and a long light box, which can be used to view slides or negatives, runs along the nearby curved wall.

Cato Gobe came up with a new dispensing "tower" for the film which also becomes a focal point. To segment the films and "explain" their differences, each tower displays a photograph taken with the particular film contained in and dispensed from that tower.

The original name, Rahola, is applied over the doorway in traditional Kodak typeface. To project a "sense of creativity," Image Center is in script and accented by the curved red line which "combines a feeling of technology meshed with creativity."

INCREDIBLE UNIVERSE

Wilsonville, OR

Design: Design Forum, Dayton, OH

With 100,000 sq. ft. of selling space and 60,000 sq. ft. more of warehouse and operations space, Incredible is not a hyperbole. This is really something big! Tandy Corp. wanted a mega store for consumers — different from anything around — and Design Forum has certainly created a totally incredible, state-of-the-art, shopping experience.

Passing through the unique and imaginative store front, customers are taken "out of reality" at the registration area where they see a 21' tower flashing the energetic logo in neon lights and alive with video monitors. "Using compelling color, design, and engineering, it is the first hint of what the Incredible Universe is all about." Customers then "transition" through a 10 ft. high tunnel where the store's positioning statement is communicated through floor-to-ceiling graphics. Outside the tunnel, shoppers now find themselves surrounded by the many specialty stores set up in this monster store.

The hub of the store is an 8,000 sq. ft. rotunda with a stage in the center. This is a "core of pure excitement, and features hands-on demonstrations, educational programs, celebrity appearances and presentations by manufacturer representatives." Suspended from the ceiling is the Diamond Vision Jumbo-Tron.

Incredible Universe is set up like a mall and each "store" in it conveys its identity in its own special fashion. The massive scale and the neon accents of the signage increase that sense of excitement and provides additional animation. The signs are really over-sized sculptures that assist shoppers in identifying the store's product line.

The Big Store which surrounds the rotunda has 350 TV models, 90 models of VCRs and much, much more. It offers customers a wall two stories high and 100 ft. wide that is filled with television sets. The architecture of the Big Store contains catwalks and exposed structures which are integrated with strong lighting and bright graphics while capitalizing on its warehouse identity.

This store is designed to be "the future" and it responds with the biggest and best selection of appliances, audio equipment, videos and computer software — at competitive prices — in the world. Incredible? Awesome!

STAR FACTORY

Gurnee Mills S/C, Gurnee, IL

Design: Florian / Wierzbowski Designs, Chicago, IL
Paul Florian & Stephen Wierzbowski
Project Director: Robin Whitehurst
Graphic Design: Lora Delestowicz
Photographer: Steve Hall & Heidrich Blessing, Chicago, IL

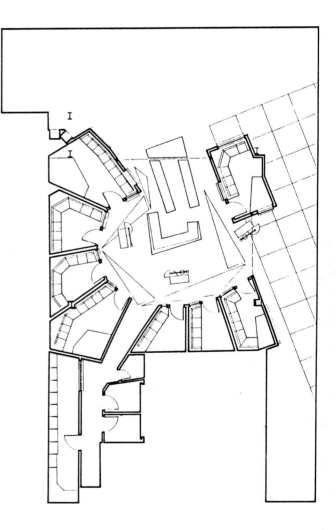

Karaoke, the Japanese sing-along phenomenon has also grown in popularity in the U.S. It is a fad that has caught on and for those would-be "pop" or "rock" stars and their "groups" who want to, they can now go down to the mall — enclose themselves in small rooms and sing along with the vocal-less arrangement of current tunes. The Japanese company, Pioneer Laser Entertainment, has entered the market here in the U.S. and in addition to "singing," the "star" now gets a recording on tape or a CD of the performance.

The 2,600 sq. ft. Karaoke store in the Gurnee Mills S/C was designed by the Chicago design firm, Florian Wierzbowski. The Star Factory is the first in this country and it consists of eight karaoke boxes (or studios) organized in a roughly radial pattern around a central control desk. To create the "romantic dream" of what a recording studio might be like, the designers used a bright palette of red, yellow and black — of stars on the studio doors — and heavily grained birch veneer plywood walls that are meant to suggest "an architecture of musical instruments." Metal meshes, theater lights, exposed acoustical materials and banks of video monitors lend the space a high-tech, glamourous "backstage" ambience.

The customer in the studio selects a song and goes through several "rehearsals." When the performer is ready, he/she signals the engineer who is located in the central control booth and visible through the double paned glass windows. The engineer then cues up the machinery and records. "This interplay between customer and engineer — with machinery as the connection — enriches and humanizes the experience of entertainment technology."

Located within the space is also a small "store" where souvenirs appropriate to the experience can be purchased.

THE WALL

Roosevelt Field, Garden City, NY

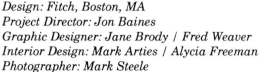

Design: Fitch, Boston, MA
Project Director: Jon Baines
Graphic Designer: Jane Brody / Fred Weaver
Interior Design: Mark Arties / Alycia Freeman
Photographer: Mark Steele

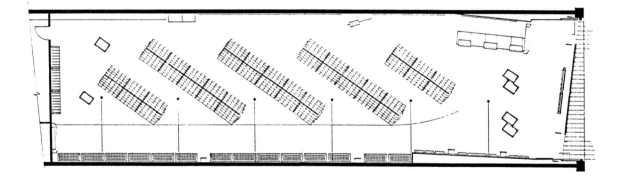

Over the years, the W.H. Smith company has acquired several existing regional music stores and now they commissioned Fitch of Boston to create a single retail brand identity for The Wall. In addition, the design and graphics firm was asked to turn The Wall into a "branded retail destination differentiated from other mall record stores."

Most of the stores vary from 3,500 sq. ft. to 7,000 sq. ft. and Fitch designed an innovative store layout "derived from an arcing primary pathway which established a circulation pattern that draws shoppers to the rear of the store." Shoppers can browse along a walkway with "off-ramps" for exiting to musical areas by type or classification.

The design solution began with the dynamic angular store front design which interrupts the usual symmetry found in store facias in malls. "Architectural details related to changes in lighting and flooring materials, varying ceiling heights, and related ancillary textures and finishes, add drama to the space and help to define the functional areas."

A retail visual identity, drawn from a graphic palette based on the electromagnetic spectrum, acts as an integral part of the design concept and it unites the store's look from shelf edge to bags to signs and tags. "Its kinetic color elements and graphic figures enabled design variations within a single theme — flexibility which led to a spectral color scheme for segmenting musical genres."

VIRGIN MEGASTORE

Hamburg, Germany

Design: RSCG Conran Design, London, England
Design Team: Tim Greenhalgh / Tom Redpath
Photographer: Nicholas Gentilli

With two stories and 20,000 sq. ft. of space, this is the largest Virgin Megastore in Germany. Located in Hamburg and designed by the London based firm, RSCG Conran Design, the store's design is typical of the Megastore profile: "Youthful, bright and exciting while remaining knowledgeable, authoritative and specialist."

The extensively glazed, double height store front was kept uncluttered which in effect maximized both the amount of natural light and the viewing into the store. A large void was incorporated above the entrance which allows shoppers to see through to the upper floor as it creates a feeling of spaciousness. Inside the store each department has its own distinctive look. The Rock/Pop/Video areas are alive with bright blue and orange paint finishes and restrained by the sandstone linoleum on the floor. The same colors — this time with geometric patterned floors — appear in the games section which spills out into the main walkway.

The bottle green and red walls and beams of the Jazz department are accentuated by uplighting while the Classical area is more serene and formal with a deep red carpet and American cherry wood fixtures. Here the lighting is focused and subdued. Dramatic staircases connect the two levels of the store.

ABOUT THE EDITOR

Martin M. Pegler has long been considered a leading authority on store design and visual merchandising. He has been involved in the field for almost forty years and has worked in all phases of merchandise presentation: designer, manufacturer, display person, store planner and consultant. Witty, urbane, erudite and most persuasive, he has long been a vocal champion of store design and visual presentation as a necessary and respected part of retailing. This has made him a popular speaker across the country and for two tours of the British Isles, Mexico and Japan. He is in demand as a lecturer for industry, small business groups as well as, nation-wide chains and shopping centers.

Mr. Pegler is author of *Successful Food Merchandising & Display, Stores of the Year, Store Windows That Sell, Food Presentation & Display, Home Furnishings Merchandising & Store Design,* and *Market Supermarket & Hypermarket Design.*

He is currently a professor of Store Planning and Visual Merchandising at the Fashion Institute of Technology in New York and travels extensively, — always searching the field for new and fresh approaches, ideas and techniques to share.